Man's Accidents and God's Purposes

JAMES K. FOLSOM is presently an instructor in English and American Studies at Yale University. After completing his undergraduate degree at Northwestern University, he studied in Austria and subsequently received the Ph.D. from Princeton University. He has collaborated with Willard Thorp, Carlos Baker, and Merle Curti on an anthology of American literature and is the author of a number of literary studies. At present he is engaged in writing a critical history of the "Western" from Natty Bumppo to Matt Dillon.

Man's Accidents
and
God's Purposes

Multiplicity in Hawthorne's Fiction

by

James K. Folsom

COLLEGE AND UNIVERSITY PRESS
263 Chapel Street   **New Haven, Conn.**

Copyright © 1963 by College and University Press

Library of Congress Catalog Card Number: 63-8498

MANUFACTURED IN THE UNITED STATES OF AMERICA BY
UNITED PRINTING SERVICES, INC.
NEW HAVEN, CONN.

FOR BOBBY

Acknowledgments

I would like to express my general thanks to all who have helped me in the course of writing this study and of doing the research for it, most particularly to my friends, who *would* often listen to Hawthorneana, their own desires notwithstanding. Specific thanks are due to the staff of the Princeton University library, most especially to Mr. Malcolm Young, former reference librarian there, for bibliographical help; to Professor Willard Thorp of Princeton and to Professors Charles Feidelson and R. W. B. Lewis of Yale who read the manuscript at various stages in its development, though the author's vagaries are not accountable to them; to the Yale University Graduate School for a grant in aid which enabled me to have the final draft of the manuscript re-typed; and to Mrs. Brian McMahon for typing it.

I am deeply indebted as well to Professor Lawrance Thompson of Princeton, who first directed my attention to Hawthorne as a subject of study, and who later patiently helped me with the early drafts of this book; and to Professor Norman Holmes Pearson of Yale, who has been a constant friend in need during the final stages of preparation of the manuscript.

J. K. F.

New Haven, Connecticut
January, 1963

Contents

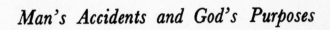

Man's Accidents and God's Purposes

I

The Nature of Reality

IN 1843, on one of the windows of the Old Manse, Sophia
Hawthorne scratched with a diamond an apparently commonplace maxim: "Man's accidents are God's purposes."[1] This
rather platitudinous axiom represents, in capsule form, a commonplace of nineteenth-century metaphysical thought, here
given expression in terms of some type of divine Providence,
namely that God is in His nature unknowable to man, although
man's actions reflect, in some mysterious way, His purposes.
Sophia Hawthorne's short statement very aptly summarizes
Hawthorne's own attitude toward the relation between God and
man, or, to expand the definition, between ultimate Reality
and reality as it is knowable in its finite, experiential forms.
Father Leonard Fick has shown that "the keystone . . . of Hawthorne's theology is an unshakable belief in an inscrutable Providence,"[2] which, although Hawthorne does not apparently equate
it with God, is certainly God as He is manifest in this world. As
B. Bernard Cohen points out, "Hawthorne's God is Inscrutable.
Man must not attempt to fathom the mysteries of His actions,
but instead must trust to His kindness,"[3] and this trust, for
Hawthorne, takes the form of blind reliance on a Providence
whose workings man is unable to comprehend. For purposes of
the following discussion the inscrutability of this Providence is
what must be insisted upon, the idea that God's purposes are
unknowable except insofar as they are visible through their
workings, man's accidents. The philosophical position which
underlies this maxim—if we can inflate it enough to dignify its
content with the name of philosophy—is a commonplace Christian one as it is stated here, and basically probably a very loosely
Platonic one. It assumes two "worlds," that of Man's accidents,

13

which can be empirically known, and some ultimate Real world, that of God's purposes, which is inscrutable in itself but upon which the former world depends. But, as Hawthorne uses the concept, its differences from orthodox Platonism in any form are much more striking than its similarities. The Platonist has always been concerned with the world of Purpose, the world of God, the world of Reality; Hawthorne, conversely, is fascinated by the world of Accident, of Man, of Appearance, although always admitting the dependence of this world of Experience upon some transcendental Reality. Nevertheless, although this transcendental world, this ultimate Reality, is the only principle of ultimate validity, it cannot in its very nature be known except as it is manifest in the everyday world of Appearance.

The inscrutability of this world of ultimate Reality and the impossibility of any knowledge of it on the part of man is basic to Hawthorne's artistic and philosophical vision. He himself used the maxim which his wife had scratched on the window of the Old Manse in a completely serious context some nineteen years later. In "Chiefly About War Matters," which contains, along with his *Life of Franklin Pierce,* most of his serious opinions about the Civil War and the problem of slavery, he uses the phrase in a nonfictional context to draw a possible providential moral. He, with some other visitors to Washington, had been taken to see some Confederate prisoners incarcerated at Harpers Ferry. His reflections upon them were not of the usual order; he had neither a feeling of jingoistic self-satisfaction for the success of Northern arms nor was he overcome by a conventional mood of sentimental humanitarianism, that these poor prisoners were like their captors under their different uniforms. Rather he reflected that the captives represented a human type which he had supposed nonexistent in the United States, although he had learned to know it in Europe—the peasant. He concludes his ruminations over the prisoners somewhat moralistically:

> Looking round at these poor prisoners, therefore, it
> struck me as an immense absurdity that they should fancy
> us their enemies; since, whether we intend it so or no, they
> have a far greater stake on our success than we can possibly

have. For ourselves, the balance of advantages between defeat and triumph may admit of question. For them, all truly valuable things are dependent on our complete success; for thence would come the regeneration of a people,—the removal of a foul scurf that has overgrown their life, and keeps them in a state of disease and decrepitude, one of the chief symptoms of which is, that, the more they suffer and are debased, the more they imagine themselves strong and beautiful. *No human effort, on a grand scale, has ever yet resulted according to the purpose of its projectors. The advantages are always incidental. Man's accidents are God's purposes. We miss the good we sought, and do the good we little cared for* [italics mine].[4]

The italicized conclusion to this passage is worthy of note. In it Hawthorne makes a serious, general statement about the relation of God to man, of Reality to Appearances. Man's accidents are here truly accidental. Indeed, when man attempts to mold his efforts into the direction which he conceives to be that of Providence he succeeds only in furthering the mysterious ends of Providence by means of completely different results from those he had anticipated. Nevertheless, and this point needs emphasis as well as the preceding, because the world of Purpose works its inscrutable will through the world of Appearances does not mean that there *is* no world of Purpose or of God. Hawthorne is explicit in his belief that there are two worlds, and that they are interdependent; but he insists, as well, that we have knowledge of only one of them, the world of Appearances.

Hawthorne emphasizes this point again in his discussion of Negro slavery in the *Life of Franklin Pierce.* Hawthorne's position on the slavery question was always anti-Abolitionist, not because he thought that slavery was morally justifiable, but because he felt that it was an evil which did not exist in itself, but was symptomatic of a radical imperfection in the nature of man. In the *Life of Franklin Pierce* he opposes "another view" which, he says, is "probably as wise a one" to the cherished Abolitionist tenet that the evils of slavery could be abolished by legislative *fiat* combined, if necessary, with military force. Hawthorne's other view is not so simple. This view "looks upon slavery as one of those evils which divine Providence does not leave to be remedied by human contrivances, but which, in its own good time, by some means impossible to be anticipated, but of the simplest and easiest operation, when all its uses shall have been fulfilled, it causes to vanish like a dream." Man's accidents are God's purposes here with a vengeance. But Hawthorne goes on to draw a more specific moral: "There is no instance, in all history, of the human will and intellect having perfected any great moral reform by methods which it adapted to that end; but the progress of the world, at every step, leaves some evil or wrong on the path behind it, which the wisest of mankind, of their own set purpose, could never have found the way to rectify."[5]

The point of Hawthorne's attack on the Abolitionists here is that their explanation of the cause of slavery is too facile. One must realize, Hawthorne is saying, that slavery is not merely an inexplicable blot on the reputation of the southern states, but a symptom of a basic flaw in the human character as well. It is only logical, he says, to assume that the abolishing of one evil will be followed by the establishment of another. Slavery, one might say, is a necessary evil, not in the economic sense that slaves are needed to do the menial work on plantations, but in the sense that it is a symptom of an underlying imperfection in man's character. If man's character is purified sufficiently, slavery will vanish like a dream; but until that time comes it is useless to attempt its abolition. To meddle in the concerns of Providence is futile, Hawthorne says in effect, because slavery is a symptom of an unpleasant Reality which we do not understand. Those who believe that slavery can be abolished by legislative action fail to see that slavery is not self-existent, but rather symptomatic of an inherent fault in the nature of man. The only way to eliminate the Apparent evil of slavery, Hawthorne points out, is to change the Essential evil of men, and when this is done slavery will disappear of its own accord. But, he insists, we cannot change this Essential evil by striking at its Apparent manifestations.

One might well ask at this point whence Hawthorne derived this loosely Platonic dualism. To this question one must answer,

I think, that he could have learned it in many places. J. P. Pritchard has shown that there is very little evidence of any direct influence on Hawthorne by Aristotle or Horace, even though he studied Horace, at least, at Bowdoin.[6] Direct influences on Hawthorne are usually traced to three main sources: the Puritans, the Transcendentalists, and the Romantics. Most studies of these sources show either that Hawthorne was not wholly of any party or else that he could have learned a given thing from any one source.

Actually, each of these general groups depends upon a loosely dualistic Platonic philosophy, that is, on a belief that the world of experience is a type of some super-experiential reality. If, as H. W. Schneider suggests, the Puritans' "whole sense of values and perspective of imagination . . . were dominated by their belief in the literal reality of the invisible world,"[7] so was Hawthorne's. The Transcendentalists' view, whether carefully explicated in Hegelian logic or metaphorically expressed in Emerson's transparent eyeball was, in Hawthorne's sense, expressive of a loosely Platonic relationship between the real and apparent worlds. And the English Romantics, ranging roughly from the immanent theism of Wordsworth to the closely reasoned metaphoric Platonism of Shelley, held in common a belief in the integral relation of the Apparent and the Real worlds.[8] Therefore, we must conclude, if only through the immense weight of contradictory evidence, that Hawthorne could have learned his Platonic world-view from many sources; that he learned it from *one* source is very doubtful. His own comment on the "sources" of Shakespeare's philosophy which Delia Bacon found in Sir Francis Bacon's writings applies to his own case as well. He writes to Delia Bacon:

> I cannot say, at present, that I adopt your theory, if I rightly comprehend it as partially developed in this portion of your work. We find thoughts in all great writers (and even in small ones) that strike their roots far beneath the surface, and intertwine themselves with the roots of other writers' thoughts; so that when we pull up one, we stir the whole, and yet those writers have had no conscious society with one another.[9]

This discussion of Hawthorne's belief in Providence in a nonfictional context has, I hope, emphasized that Hawthorne never assumes that he can understand the workings of divine Providence. He is under no illusions that, because he believes in Providence, and because for him the Apparent world posits the existence of some world of ultimate Reality, this gives him any insight into its operation. His knowledge of the providential world of Being, in other words, is purely metaphorical knowledge which Hawthorne uses to explain the world of Becoming. This world of Becoming suggests the world of Being, but the world of Becoming is the only world of which even a tentative knowledge is possible. This conception of the world of Becoming as the only knowable aspect of reality finds expression in many of Hawthorne's various tales, some of which have been interpreted, in my opinion quite wrongly, as didactic ethical or metaphysical statements.

Critics have often been hard put to explain the role which the ethical dimension plays in Hawthorne's fiction. They have generally assumed one of two opposing points of view. On the one hand, Hawthorne is seen as a writer of didactic fiction, of ethical parables; on the other, his art is interpreted as being purposely vague or, to use a perhaps overworked critical term, "ambiguous." This tension has been uneasily recognized by most of Hawthorne's critics, who have tended quite often either to deplore his vagueness from the standpoint that a writer should say what he means or, conversely, have deplored his didacticism from the critical position that art, to imitate life, should be purposely vague and ambiguous. Thus, for example, Professor John W. Bicknell, in a recent criticism of *The Marble Faun*,[10] decides that the novel's failure is due to Hawthorne's unwillingness or inability to face the question squarely of whether Donatello's fall *is* or *is not* fortunate. What Professor Bicknell wishes from Hawthorne is an unequivocal statement that the fall *is* fortunate, and he is rather miffed because none is to be found in the novel. F. O. Matthiessen, in his famous stricture on Hawthorne's insistence on the reality of Faith's pink ribbon in "Young Goodman Brown," has taken just the opposite side. Here, he says, Hawthorne's "literal insistence on that damaging pink ribbon obtrudes the labels of a confining allegory and short circuits the range of associations."[11]

No one would deny that both points of view have a good deal to be said for them. Hawthorne does at times seem to write *exempla*, apparently simple moralities which appear—albeit often deceptively—to be explicable in terms of some simple ethical concept, if we only knew exactly which one. And certainly any reader of just a few of Hawthorne's tales knows that he does write ambiguously, and apparently with some purpose. That is, his ambiguity is intentional, not bad craftsmanship or careless revision.

I suggest that these two opposing views of Hawthorne's art can be reconciled if we are careful to divorce his own moral, religious, ethical and philosophical preoccupations from his aesthetic principles. We then see that Hawthorne uses ethical and moral concepts in a way analogous to the "ambiguity" of his symbols. That is, he uses alternative moral and ethical explanations of his symbols to heighten the possible interpretations of a given phenomenon. The moral dimension of Hawthorne's art, in other words, becomes an aesthetic means to suggest the multiplicity of motives and explanations inherent in any human action, yet this moral dimension is purposely divorced from any final interpretation in terms of an ultimate Reality. Rather than writing *exempla* which make an ethical point, he uses ethical concepts in quite an opposite fashion—to add to the diversity of plausible explanations of any event and to suggest the myriad interpretations possible of any apparently simple action.

This is not to deny in any fashion the validity of Hawthorne's philosophical views, or to suggest superciliously that he was at his best when he wrote "Art" and not "Ideas," or to take a common critical escape route by dividing up his personality and suggesting that he wrote some tales off the top of his mind, while other, more serious (and doubtless more worth-while) stories represent the "real" Hawthorne, the serious artist. It is rather to propose that a great deal of confusion can be avoided by a fairly close attention to terms, by an attempt to clarify the role which the moral or ethical dimension plays in Hawthorne's fiction. It is to suggest that the morality and the ethic in Hawthorne's work are handled by him in such a manner that he may demonstrate ethical ideas and moral choices and paths of conduct without ever having to suggest as an artist that these various ethical choices which his characters face—the moral crossroads at which they find themselves—give him any insight into the nature of morality in general, or into any ultimate justification for any particular moral choice considered out of the context of the particular tale in which it may occur.

Where ethical readings of Hawthorne's fiction generally go wrong is by proceeding on the assumption that in any given tale or novel some character is Hawthorne's mouthpiece, or that some ethical choice made by a character is that particular one which Hawthorne recommends. Thus, most of the criticism of *The Marble Faun*, for example, boils down to a rather fruitless and heated argument over whose explanation of the meaning of Donatello's crime we are to accept. Is the Fall fortunate, as Miriam suggests? Or in Donatello's fall are we damnéd all, as the pious and orthodox Hilda would have it?

In the controversy which is still raging over this problem of interpretation, I think it not out of place to suggest that one central bit of evidence which ought to be taken into account is that Hawthorne nowhere endorses either position in any fashion which might be construed as an *ex cathedra* utterance. If we wish to assume that the novel is an impassioned plea for the ethical doctrine of *felix culpa*, then, of course, Miriam's position is correct and her statements can be used to buttress our position. But this is an assumption which *we* must make, and it is certainly unfair to claim that Hawthorne was of our party without his knowing it. Nowadays Hilda's position is in eclipse, and those of us—if there are any—who think that it might possibly have just a shred of rational force behind it, have gone underground. When the book was first published, however, the contrary was true, Miriam's defenders being conspicuous only by their absence. It was assumed that Hilda's explanation of the action must be correct, since Miriam's was beneath the notice of any reasonable man; and, this being so, the case could be "proved" by any number of Hilda's own statements. Again, however, the reader made the initial egotistical assumption that Hawthorne must agree with him in approving Hilda's ethical bias.

The finest example of this critical game of blind-man's buff may be seen in the various interpretations of *The Scarlet Letter*. This novel is apparently a novel of ideas; it apparently develops a consistent philosophical system; it contains many quotable lines which seem to prove Hawthorne's philosophical position; and yet, somehow, no one seems to be certain just what the ideas are or what Hawthorne's philosophy is. C. C. Walcutt has, in a brilliant analysis of the critical appraisals of *The Scarlet Letter*, discovered five different readings of the novel. These readings are, in his words, (1) the "orthodox Christian" or "orthodox Puritan" reading based on the "idea that sin is permanently warping," (2) this reading plus the concept of the "Fortunate Fall," which assumes that Dimmesdale and Hester are ultimately redeemed, (3) the "romantic reading," which depends on the idea that "society is guilty of punishing individuals who have responded to a natural urge," (4) the "transcendental" reading, a variant of the "romantic" reading, which holds that Hester and Dimmesdale were not true to each other, and that their sin lay not in their conventionally immoral love but rather in "the failure of self-reliance in the lovers' not being true to themselves" and, (5) the "relativist" readings which "concentrate upon the psychological implications of the sense of guilt."[12] All these readings are to some extent opposed to one another, yet any even casual delver into Hawthorne criticism is well aware that all have been held by reputable critics and that plausible cases have been made for each of them. Furthermore, with the partial exception of the last reading, all these various interpretations depend upon taking some one character as a representative of Hawthorne's own point of view. But this is a very dangerous assumption, for Hawthorne never claims any character as his own. Indeed, whenever he attempts to mediate between opposing points of view in the novel he ends by quietly denying that the opinions of the characters represent those of the author.[13] And, in order to suggest that his characters have only an incomplete knowledge of the meaning of the action in which they are involved, he kindly submits other possibilities of interpretation which none of them have thought of, but which are equally tenable.

To my mind the inescapable conclusion which one must draw from the apparent impossibility of pinning Hawthorne down to any one opinion is that in some way he did not want to be pinned down. The moral dimension in his art, I suggest, is a moral dimension only *in the works of art themselves,* for Hawthorne uses moral and ethical concepts not with the end in view of weighing their various merits and shortcomings in order to choose the best one, but rather with the intention of showing that each, like his "ambiguous" symbols, is only an aspect of his underlying artistic preoccupation, which is the presentation in symbolic terms of that diversity underlying the apparent unity which observers always find in their own, personal, subjective interpretation of experience. Given, in other words, a fact to interpret, Hawthorne shows ultimately that it is knowable only in terms of what people see in it or make out of it, and that this knowledge does not necessarily imply the superiority of one position to another in any absolute moral or ethical sense, but only serves to demonstrate the immense complexity inherent in what are apparently the most simple facts of experience.

A brief discussion of two of Hawthorne's seemingly more didactic stories may serve to make this point clearer. The first of these tales, "David Swan," has all the earmarks of a moral *exemplum* in fictional form. Its plot is the simple story of a young man, David Swan, who falls asleep near a fountain by the roadside while waiting for the Boston stagecoach. While sleeping, he is seen by three groups of strangers: first come an elderly merchant and his wife, who have lost a son and almost decide to adopt David; second, a young girl whom, Hawthorne suggests, he would have loved if he had only been awake to see her; and finally, two robbers who determine to kill him and steal his money, but are frightened away by a stray dog. To all of these visitors David remains impervious; and, when he hears the stagecoach coming, he wakes and, climbing aboard, continues his journey to Boston. Hawthorne concludes the tale with a rather pat moral, ending in a long rhetorical question.

Up mounted David, and bowled away merrily towards Boston, without so much as a parting glance at that fountain of dreamlike vicissitude. He knew not that a phantom of Wealth had thrown a golden hue upon its waters—nor that one of Love had sighed softly to their murmur—nor that one of Death had threatened to crimson them with his blood—all, in the brief hour since he lay down to sleep. Sleeping or waking, we hear not the airy footsteps of the strange things that almost happen. Does it not argue a superintending Providence that, while viewless and unexpected events thrust themselves continually athwart our path, there should still be regularity enough in mortal life to render foresight even partially available?[14]

The final two sentences in this conclusion are quite significant. Apparently Hawthorne wants us to answer "Yes" to the rhetorical question, and it is also fairly evident that he expects no violent disagreement from us about not knowing the things that almost happen. We should, he says, as reasonable men, admit the existence of a divine Providence, of some kind of analogical relationship between ultimate Reality and the world as we know it. Nevertheless, although we are forced to admit the existence of this providential order, in its very nature, *by definition,* we cannot hope to know anything about it except the enigmatic fact that it exists. Furthermore, throughout the story Hawthorne never suggests what possible ends Providence could have had in mind through its operations. The question of why David was allowed to sleep by an all-wise Providence is never mentioned, nor is the question of why it is better for David to go on to Boston discussed at all. Questions of the nature of the providential order, of its purpose, its ends, and even of any ultimate justification of its means are, in short, beyond the province of fictional discussion, although the fact of the *existence* of this providential relationship can be fictionally assumed.

Another twist to the Platonic metaphor with which Hawthorne is working is evident in his discussion of the two "worlds" of David Swan. In an abstract sense, the world of David Swan asleep and of David Swan awake are both equally real in the world of sense experience. But to David himself, such is not the case. He does not know the things which have almost happened, and for him they do not exist. But the fact is that they *do* exist, not only abstractly, but in the world of the story. Hawthorne refers to the three groups of intruders as "phantoms," and they are phantoms, *from David Swan's point of view*. Nevertheless, they are just as real as he is from any other. In short, Hawthorne gives us here a statement of a rather commonplace event: a young man falls asleep by a fountain while waiting for the stagecoach. He then goes on to interpret this event in terms of four different points of view—those of the visitors and of David Swan himself —each one of which is different, and each one of which is incomplete, yet each one of which is in some sense true. The actual *fact* of David's sleeping, that is, is unimportant in itself. Its meaning is developed in terms of what others make out of it, in terms of the varieties of interpretation to which it is subject.

A story with a similar theme is the probably over-discussed sketch, "Fancy's Show Box." This story begins with a definition, and the statement of an ethical problem.

> What is Guilt? A stain upon the soul. And it is a point of vast interest whether the soul may contract such stains, in all their depth and flagrancy, from deeds which may have been plotted and resolved upon, but which, physically, have never had existence. Must the fleshly hand and visible frame of man set its seal to the evil designs of the soul, in order to give them their entire validity against the sinner? Or, while none but crimes perpetrated are cognizable before an earthly tribunal, will guilty thoughts—of which guilty deeds are no more than shadows—will these draw down the full weight of a condemning sentence, in the supreme court of eternity?[15]

This is, as Neal F. Doubleday has pointed out, an expanded paraphrase of Jeremy Taylor's statement that "The act of the will alone, although no external action or event do follow, is imputed to good or evil by God and men."[16] Actually, the reference need not be so esoteric. Especially in view of one of Hawthorne's examples, Christ's statement in the Sermon on the Mount becomes more than generally relevant. "Ye have heard that it was said by them of old time, Thou shalt not commit adultery: but I say unto you, That whosoever looketh on a woman to lust after her hath committed adultery with her already in his heart" (Matthew 5:27-28). The fictional method with which Hawthorne investigates this problem is the story of a certain Mr. Smith who, though apparently the pattern of moral excellence, had actually been guilty of three crimes of intent, although none had actually been committed. He had at least considered the seduction of a young lady when a youth; while under the influence of drink, had quarreled with his best friend and tried, fortunately without success, to kill him; and finally, had almost undertaken an unjust lawsuit against three orphaned children.

These three examples, Hawthorne suggests, are only a few of the crimes of intention which Mr. Smith had contemplated, and which, even though none had ever actually been committed, caused Conscience to stab him so painfully that he awoke from the dream wherein they had appeared to him. Hawthorne then gives Mr. Smith's imaginary reply to Conscience's charges, which is, as one would suspect, based on the argument that a crime of intent and a crime actually committed are two different things. What we have, in short, is an attack on and a defense of the proposition, the two sides of the philosophical debate metaphorically presented in the persons of Conscience and Mr. Smith. Hawthorne concludes the tale, however, not by deciding in favor of either party, but by postponing the question.

> . . . with the slight fancy work which we have framed, some sad and awful truths are interwoven. Man must not disclaim his brotherhood, even with the guiltiest, since, though his hand be clean, his heart has surely been polluted by the flitting phantoms of iniquity. He must feel that, when he shall knock at the gate of heaven, no semblance of an un-spotted life can entitle him to entrance there. Penitence must kneel, and Mercy come from the footstool of the throne, or that golden gate will never open![17]

The rather conventionally Christian element in this conclusion, —that man cannot presume to be just in the sight of God, but must hope for divine mercy—tends to obscure the more significant philosophical point that Hawthorne has refused to commit himself to an answer of the question he raised. He does not decide in favor either of Conscience or of Mr. Smith. What he does is to propose another hypothetical consideration: *"If* the kingdom of God can be entered only by the just man, justification can be found only through God's mercy, not through man's justice." What this consideration implies, of course, is that man is in his nature unjust, that all men are guilty in some degree or other, even if only of sins of intention. But what the unalert reader is likely to pass over is the fact that while this may be true in the world of Appearances, in the world of imperfection, it gives us no insight into the world of Reality, of perfection. Yes, man is imperfect; yes, we are all guilty in the sight of God; but no, on the basis of this information we cannot tell whether Conscience or Mr. Smith is correct. Both points of view are true in that both are logically tenable and represent positions which are held by men; but which one is correct in terms of a higher truth Hawthorne refuses to answer.

Hawthorne's insistence upon the strictly analogical relationship between the worlds of Being and Becoming finds further expression in his preoccupation with the possibility of the reordering of experience to conform more closely to some other criterion than the accidental qualifications of conventional human arrangements. A very good example of this sort of reorganization may be seen in the semi-allegorical sketch, "The Procession of Life." In this sketch, Hawthorne rejects the conventional ordering of humanity in accord with "merest external circumstances" in order to attempt to discover a "true classification."[18] Hawthorne accordingly substitutes for what he considers a superficial system of classification an arrangement based on the principles of sickness, intellect, sorrow, crime, love (i.e., benevolence), and finally the principle of misplacement, by which he means the negative classification of those who have lost, or have never found, their proper place in the world. Indeed, at the very beginning of the tale Hawthorne takes exception to conventional principles of arrangement on the grounds that life is a "festal or funereal procession" under the direction of a "Chief Marshal" who, at the end of the tale, turns out to be " Death."[19]

This is, I suppose, fairly good lugubrious graveyard doctrine, but it is more than a convention in Hawthorne's mind. Life, as Hawthorne sees it in this story, is a movement toward the Ideal world of Death. The irony of human endeavor, as Hawthorne interprets it, is that it directs its course toward temporal values while ignoring eternal ones, at least as reflected in our earthly existence. Again, the conventionally Christian conclusion may cause the unwary reader to miss the important point that the nature of the Ideal world is never stated. Life is, Hawthorne says, a movement toward death and toward a place where temporal imperfections are explicable in terms of a higher Unity. Nevertheless, although we have an analogical knowledge of this fact, this gives us no insight into the nature of the world of Unity. And although the Grand Marshal may be Death, still the principles of organization along the line of march are not eternal principles. They are, at least as they are manifest in this world, temporal principles. Although they may be psychologically sounder than the accidental and conventional classifications which they replace, they do not partake directly of any eternal verity. Rather than being a unifying insight into the confused mass of humanity, they are really a way of implying more diversity of it. Hawthorne superimposes his own system of organization upon an older one, which for his purposes is inexact, but which nevertheless has some validity. In addition to classifying mankind according to wealth, he suggests that we also consider sickness; instead of social position, intellect; and so on. The *also* is very important; for what Hawthorne is doing is giving us two possible ways of looking at mankind, two possible different classifications of identical phenomena.

This ordering of experience in terms of some other principle is often expressed in terms of the *Bildungsroman* in which Hawthorne typically initiates the protagonist constantly more deeply into the meaning of truth. Hawthorne is quite capable of treating this serious theme in an apparently comic manner, as he does in at least two often under-praised stories, "Mr. Higginbotham's Catastrophe" and "Mrs. Bullfrog." In the first of these stories Dominicus Pike, a traveling peddler, is given information that one Mr. Higginbotham has been murdered "by an Irishman and a nigger."[20] He retells this story as he goes along his route, only to be apparently proven wrong by indubitable facts presented to him by his auditors. Eventually, however, he comes on Mr. Higginbotham who is just about to be murdered, and he is able at one stroke to save Mr. Higginbotham's life and to vindicate his own sources of information. Hawthorne appends a note at the end of the tale to clarify its plot for those whom the somewhat tangled skein of events has mystified.

I do not wish to impale a deep moral significance on this rather offhand story, but still the tale is, I think, worthy of more notice than it has hitherto received. The basic conflict in the tale lies in the question of the primacy of two orders of truth, represented on the one hand by the apparently unimpeachable evidence of those who know for a fact that Mr. Higginbotham is alive and well, and on the other by Dominicus Pike, who on the basis of apparently untrustworthy opinion believes Mr. Higginbotham to have been murdered. Both of these opinions ultimately prove to be false when Dominicus frustrates Mr. Higginbotham's murderer. Yet Dominicus Pike's idea of the truth is closer to the "real" truth than is the apparently unimpeachable evidence of the multitude, just as Hepzibah and Clifford Pyncheon's view of Jaffrey's character is more in accord with the real facts of the case than is the view of the populace of Massachusetts. In short, as a study of modes of perception, the tale can be quite closely compared with "The Prophetic Pictures,"[21] being a kind of comic probing of the same theme there developed more seriously. It should be emphasized again, however, that the truth which Dominicus Pike perceives is not the Truth of the world of Being. Rather, he is possessed of a mode of explaining a certain happening which appears to be incorrect, although it is ultimately vindicated. Those who say Mr. Higginbotham has not been murdered and Dominicus Pike, who insists that he has been, are working on premises which they think to be true. Indeed, both premises *are* in a sense true, yet both are different and, more significantly, each point of view, although incomplete, is inescapable if one follows the premises of each argument. The answer to the question of whether or not Mr. Higginbotham has been murdered depends upon the acceptance of testimonial evidence. Whose witnesses, in short, are lying, Dominicus Pike's or those of the community at large? Significantly, *all* are telling the truth to the best of their ability, but since none is in a position to know all the facts, his testimony is, without his knowing it, somewhat distorted. Again we see two opposite interpretations of a single event, each one of which is partially incomplete and yet is not wholly false.

"Mrs. Bullfrog" is at once a more obvious and more easily interpreted example. Though this tale has alway been looked at somewhat askance by critics, it has on occasion received its share of comment, usually of somewhat undue solemnity. B. Bernard Cohen takes the story seriously as "a satire on marriage based solely on money." He concludes that "Mr. Bullfrog is willing to overlook his wife's bad traits—and they are immense— so long as her dowry is sufficient. There is no genuine love between them; it is a perverted marriage based entirely on dollars and cents."[22] Malcolm Cowley has darkly hinted that the story is typical of a certain narcissistic strain in Hawthorne's character[23] and, of course, the tale is a prime example of Hawthorne's often rather pungent commentaries upon woman in general. Another possible interpretation, however, is that this tale is a comic probing of how Mr. Froggie went a'courting and what he found.

Mr. Bullfrog, speaking as a sadder and wiser man at the beginning of the tale, tells us how as a youth he had, in common with other "fools," paid "a most undue attention to little niceties" of personal appearance, habits, disposition, and other trifles. He moralizes sententiously that "an unhappy gentleman, resolving to wed nothing short of perfection, keeps his heart and hand till both get so old and withered that no tolerable woman will accept them," concluding flatly that "this is the very height of absurdity."[24] Mr. Bullfrog himself had almost made this mistake when courting, but had been saved from it by the inscrutable wisdom of a divine Providence acting through the somewhat unlikely finite agency of a court of law. Mr. Bullfrog, of course, has not by any means recognized the ideal in womanhood; like any seeker after it—Aylmer, for example, in "The Birthmark"—he has been disappointed. He has, though, received one valuable bit of education: that in this world the ideal is unobtainable.

Mr. Bullfrog, realizing that his ideal is unattainable, accepts a compromise in the form of five thousand dollars which Mrs. Bullfrog has won in a breach of promise suit and which he uses to set himself up in business.[25]

This result, at first glance, does not seem to be a change for the better, Mr. Bullfrog having, at least superficially, merely exchanged one unworthy end for another. And this gives some credit at least to Professor Cohen's reading of the story. Still, such a reading misses the tone of the tale—and the fact that Bullfrog has at least had an educational experience which we, as readers, may profit from even if he cannot. Actually, in his comic, fumbling, and only too human way Mr. Bullfrog has made the best of what would appear to be an almost hopeless situation, and his triumph has been greater in that it was accomplished only at the sacrifice of a cherished, though unrealistic, ideal. The acceptance of the five thousand dollars is a symbolic acceptance of the facts of the imperfections of this earthly state; the man whom Mr. Bullfrog supplanted in Mrs. Bullfrog's affections lost his ideal and his five thousand dollars as well. Providential workings, here as throughout Hawthorne's works, are inscrutable, and Mr. Bullfrog has no more insight into them at the end of the tale than he had at the beginning.

A parallel serio-comic statement of Mr. Bullfrog's predicament may be found in Hawthorne's "Spectator," in an editorial plea for funds. He reminds his readers that "in order to carry on any enterprise with spirit, MONEY is absolutely nescessary [sic]. Money, although it is the root of all evil, is also the foundation of almost everything great and good, and therefore, if our Subscribers would wish to see the Spectator flourish, they will please carefully to remember, that the terms are 2 cents pr. month."[26]

A similar point is made by the enigmatic chorus at the end of The House of the Seven Gables. As the family leaves the old house to establish themselves elsewhere, "two men" comment upon the action, emblematic of the course of events in the book as a whole.

This principle is not necessarily a pleasant one; in Hawthorne's more didactic tales, for example "The Procession of Life," the principle is Death, and in Young Goodman Brown it is Evil. Just what the principle is in "Major Molyneux" is never really clarified except metaphorically. Robin becomes like God, knowing good and evil, and signifies his new knowledge by mysterious laughter. The laughter, in this tale, like the Black Mass in "Young Goodman Brown," has an inverse sacramental quality, or at least is capable of a sacramental definition: it is an outward and visible sign of an inward and spiritual grace. For Hawthorne seems to feel with the medieval schoolmen that man is a rational animal, mortal *and capable of laughter.* Still, one should immediately notice that all the laughter in the climactic scene of the tale is not the same, though it rises from the same cause. F. B. Newman has pointed out the difference in kind between Robin's laughter and the laughter of the townspeople. The townspeople's laughter "obviously stands for our common human glee at the disillusionment of the pure in spirit" but Robin's laughter is different. "Surely it is not at the plight of Major Molyneux. Nor does it seem likely that he laughs at the fondness of his own youthful hopes." Yet Newman's conclusion, that Robin's laughter is the laughter of "hysteria," is in my opinion incorrect.[28] Robin's laughter, it seems to me, is louder because Robin has seen more deeply into the meaning of Major Molyneux's degradation. As in the other tales, the story resolves itself into a statement of perception into a hidden meaning which is stated only metaphorically and subjectively, as it is understood by the characters in the story. The townspeople laugh loud; Robin laughs louder; Major Molyneux does not laugh at all.[29]

The reader may object that this discussion of the pattern of the *Bildungsroman* in Hawthorne's fiction has taken us rather far from a purely aesthetic discussion of Hawthorne's artistic principles, but I do not think it is really beside the point, if only because it serves to show how the aesthetic and the moral are inextricably entwined in Hawthorne's art, and how each is purposely divorced from any explanation in terms of any ultimate Reality. Man's accidents are God's purposes in the realm of artistic meaning as well as in the realm of artistic form, and beauty is truth in both a moral and an aesthetic frame of reference; but this gives us only an analogical insight into the unknown and unknowable nature of transcendental Beauty and Truth. As Frederick Crews has so brilliantly shown in his analysis of *The Blithedale Romance,* Hawthorne's definition of the Unpardonable Sin as "the separation of the intellect from the heart" forms not only the basis for the book's meaning, but for its formal structure as well.[30] How Hawthorne's moral and aesthetic views shade into each other may be very nicely seen by comparing "The Great Stone Face" with "Drowne's Wooden Image."

"The Great Stone Face" is the story of a legend, told in a valley of the White Mountains, that "at some future day" a child would be born in the valley "who was destined to become the greatest and noblest personage of his time, and whose countenance, in manhood, should bear an exact resemblance to the Great Stone Face."[31] In the course of the story, resemblances are seen between the Face and Mr. Gathergold, a merchant, Old Blood-and-Thunder, a general, Old Stony Phiz, a politician, and finally a poet. Each of these fancied resemblances ultimately proves false, yet the prophecy is fulfilled through the agency of a young man named Ernest—an intentional pun—who, through his wisdom, becomes the earthly counterpart of the Great Stone Face and whose face at last resembles it. The Platonic image of the Great Stone Face's reproduction in the human face of Ernest is proof of what Hawthorne was attempting; the old theme of different modes of perception may be seen in the order of the perception of the meaning of the Face by the various characters, each of whom more closely resembles it than his predecessor, and each of whom comes closer to an understanding of its significance. Hawthorne has also come as close as he ever does to an explicit statement of the relation of the Ideal to its earthly expression; but again the metaphorical quality of this statement should be insisted upon. Ernest has somehow attained to a perception of the meaning in the enigmatic Face, but what his perception is we are never told, and its unknowability is further emphasized by Ernest's steadfast refusal to admit his likeness to the Great Stone Face.

"Drowne's Wooden Image," on the other hand, is a perhaps over-explicit statement of Hawthorne's beliefs about the relation of the Ideal to the artist and to his work. Drowne, a figurehead maker, once in his life creates a genuine work of art. Normally his figures are dull and pedestrian, but one of them is truly beautiful, an image which partakes of the Ideal form he discerned in its model and which, even in disregard of merely mechanical rules, expresses this Ideal form. Copley, the artist, who throughout the story acts as a commentator upon the action and upon artistic endeavor generally, says, after seeing Drowne's model, "You have been a truly fortunate man. What painter or statuary ever had such a subject! No wonder that she inspired a genius into you, *and first created the artist who afterwards created her image* [italics mine]."[32] In other words Drowne has not been copying a woman but an ideal form which he saw expressed in a particular model and which he succeeded in capturing in his wooden image.

The analogue which I would like to emphasize here is not that of Drowne to Ernest, but rather that of Drowne's figurehead to Ernest's wisdom. Both Ernest and Drowne have, Ernest through his life and Drowne through his art, produced something in accord with the Ideal which each has imitated. Ernest's Ideal has produced wisdom; Drowne's, art, yet the two products are remarkably similar. The poet, listening to Ernest, discovers that beauty and truth are really one, for he realizes "that the being and character of Ernest were a nobler strain of poetry than he had ever written."[33] Presumably, in this story there is only one Ideal form for both truth and beauty, and it is significant that to Hawthorne's mind the manifestations of this Ideal are decidedly different, albeit analogous. The explanation of diverse phenomena in terms of an Ideal form has again been a means to multiply effects rather than to explain the Unity which lies behind them. The mysteriousness of the Ideal which has been copied in both stories must be insisted upon. Had Drowne only copied a woman, the problem would be quite easy—but he has not. He has copied the Ideal which he, and he alone, has seen expressed in his model, and which to us is unknowable except as we perceive it expressed in his wooden image.

Not sufficient critical notice has been given to the fact that Hawthorne's studies of the artist are not a complete discussion of the problems of artistic creation, since they do not attempt to answer the question of how the artist actually creates a work of art. Hawthorne is uncompromisingly silent on this point, which is, after all, of some importance. If art is an imitation of ideal beauty, one may reasonably ask how this imitation is made. The probably apocryphal story of the Roman general who angrily reprimanded a slave for carelessly handling a priceless Greek statue by threatening, "If you break that you'll stay here until you make another just like it!" is pertinent. Actually, this perhaps mythical general is making a profound statement about the nature of art. If one work of art is an imitation of a second, and this of a third, and so on, artistic endeavor may quite well be a matter of the deft handling of a chisel, at least if we do not inquire too curiously into the end of the finite series of statues. For Hawthorne, however, the act of imitation itself seems to be a creative act. Hilda, in *The Marble Faun*, is a case in point. Hawthorne goes to great trouble to assure the reader that Hilda is especially qualified as a copyist because of certain moral and aesthetic qualities which she brings with her to her task. She is able, in her copies, to re-create the genius of the original artist, so that her copies are in a sense originals. It should be emphasized that the qualities which Hilda has are not qualities which give her some kind of empathetic relationship with the subject of her pictures. She makes a wonderful copy of Guido's Beatrice Cenci, with whom either personally or imaginatively she has absolutely nothing in common. Miriam, on the other hand, who is tantalizingly identified with Beatrice Cenci throughout the book and who can appreciate the excellence of Hilda's copy, is not herself capable of creating one. The point is carefully made in Chapter VII, "Beatrice." It is notable that Miriam herself is drawn to the work of art and not to the artist, while Hilda attempts always to catch the spirit of the artist as expressed in the picture. Miriam, that is, does not possess Hilda's gift of intuitive and super-rational penetration into the nature of the Ideal. Miriam's and Hilda's comments on artistic theory are always placed in explicit contrast. Hilda's gifts as a copyist are analyzed in Chapter VI, "The Virgin's Shrine." Visitors to the galleries who saw her at work, that is, if they "had sensibility enough to understand what was before their eyes . . . soon felt inclined to believe that the spirits of the old masters were hovering over Hilda, and guiding her delicate white hand." Also, Hilda does not usually attempt a reproduction of an entire picture, but selects some "high, noble, and delicate portion of it," expressive of the "spirit and essence" of the whole picture. Indeed, she herself is often able to produce a picture which is better than that of the original artist, for she imitates his conception of the picture rather than his actual performance.

> In some instances even (at least, so those believed who best appreciated Hilda's power and sensibility) she had been enabled to execute what the great master had conceived in his imagination, but had not so perfectly succeeded in putting upon canvas; a result surely not impossible when such depth of sympathy as she possessed was assisted by the delicate skill and accuracy of her slender hand. In such cases the girl was but a finer instrument, a more exquisitely effective piece of mechanism, by the help of which the spirit of some great departed painter now first achieved his ideal, centuries after his own earthly hand, that other tool, had turned to dust.[34]

In short, Hawthorne's idea seems to be that a work of art is an imitation of an Ideal form, but not basically a purely mechanical imitation, *and not subject to rational analysis.* The method of depicting Ideal beauty is that part of the artist's relation to his art which is indisputably his own. Hilda's qualifications as a copyist are placed in implicit contrast to those of the workmen who copy a sculptor's conception from a plaster cast into marble. Hawthorne was openly critical of such effort. It is, he says, "not quite satisfactory" to think that a sculptor today does not carve his own statues. The copyists, so to speak the Aminadabs of a sculptor's studio, are possessed of "merely mechanical skill," though this is of the highest order. They can produce nothing unless a model of it is before their eyes. They are the type of slaves in which the Roman general would delight. Hawthorne damns them as "nameless machine[s] in human shape."[35]

Some more light is thrown on this part of Hawthorne's thought by the short tale "Feathertop" which, among other things, is an allegory of the creative process. Mother Rigby creates a work of art in the person of Feathertop himself, by combining the raw materials of art, in this case the stuff which scarecrows are made on, with the Ideal form of man. Mrs. Rigby's creation, like all works of art, falls far short of the artist's original view of the Ideal, though, as Hawthorne suggests throughout the story, the Ideal in this case is a remarkably shabby one. Feathertop, in short, has only a dependent existence, dependent on the pipe which Mother Rigby gives him and which Dickon, an obliging fiend, relights upon occasion by means of a coal from a supernatural fire of doubtful sanctity. At any rate, when Mother Rigby performs the act of creation Hawthorne is conscientiously explicit. Mother Rigby gives the as yet unidealized Feathertop the magical pipe with the sardonic exhortation, "Puff, darling, puff! . . . Puff away, my fine fellow! your life depends upon it!" At this point Hawthorne decides that the story is obviously entering the realm of the incredible and that some explanation of these events is called for.

> This was a strange exhortation, undoubtedly, to be addressed to a mere thing of sticks, straw, and old clothes, with nothing better than a shrivelled pumpkin for a head,— as we know to have been the scarecrow's case. Nevertheless, as we must carefully hold in remembrance, Mother Rigby was a witch of singular power and dexterity; and, keeping this fact duly before our minds, we shall see nothing beyond credibility in the remarkable incidents of our story. Indeed, the great difficulty will be at once got over, if we can only bring ourselves to believe that, as soon as the old dame bade him puff, there came a whiff of smoke from the scarecrow's mouth. It was the very feeblest of whiffs, to be sure; but it was followed by another and another, each more decided than the preceding one.[36]

As an explanation, of course, this ostentatiously solemn disquisition is worse than useless. At the same time, there is a carp of truth to be caught here in Hawthorne's implied statement that the artistic process, by which I mean the actual production of a work of art, is in its nature undiscoverable. Mother Rigby is a witch of "singular power and dexterity," and if we keep this in mind we will have no further problems. The artistic process, in short, can be seen either in the completed work of art or in the person of the artist; the art historian or critic has his choice of regarding Feathertop or of interviewing Mother Rigby; the relation between the two can be studied within strictly defined limits of cause and effect, i.e., this artist produced that work of art; any methodological questions, however, as well as any discussion of the nature of the Ideal from which the artist copied his work, must remain a mystery.

Hawthorne's view of the way in which Art imitates Reality receives expression in another general way in those stories which deal with the artist's attempt to produce a work of art, usually seen in the image of the failure of artistic performance to keep up with the artistic ideal. A good example may be found in Hilda's visit to Kenyon's studio toward the end of *The Marble Faun*, during which she compliments him on his almost completed statue of Cleopatra. Kenyon is pleased with Hilda's approbation, although he doubts whether it is deserved. He tells her: "That inevitable period has come,—for I have found it inevitable, in regard to all my works,—when I look at what I fancied to be a statue, lacking only breath to make it live, and find it a mere lump of senseless stone, into which I have not really succeeded in moulding the spiritual part of my idea. I should like, now,— only it would be such shameful treatment for a discrowned queen, and my own offspring too,—I should like to hit poor Cleopatra a bitter blow on her Egyptian nose with this mallet."[37]

The wry conclusion should not cause us to dismiss Kenyon's statement. After all, an analogous fate was in store for the Artist of the Beautiful, whose butterfly was destroyed by a thoughtless child. Yet the loss of the butterfly did not depress Owen Warland, since, as Hawthorne says, "He had caught a far other butterfly than this. When the artist rose high enough to achieve the beautiful, the symbol by which he made it perceptible to mortal senses became of little value in his eyes while his spirit possessed itself in the enjoyment of the reality."[38] This

final statement is a fit conclusion to the tale. Owen Warland
has spent—Danforth, Peter Hovenden and Annie would say
wasted—his time in pursuit of the Ideal form, only to have his
representation of it destroyed. It would appear to the careless
reader, and doubtless seemed so to Warland's only barely polite
auditors, that this was small enough reward. But Hawthorne
is not being bitter or cynical, for though the butterfly has been
destroyed, the box in which he gave it to Annie has not. This
box "was carved richly out of ebony by his own hand, and inlaid
with a fanciful tracery of pearl, representing a boy in pursuit of
a butterfly, which, elsewhere, had become a winged spirit, and
was flying heavenward; while the boy, or youth, had found
such efficacy in his strong desire that he ascended from earth
to cloud, and from cloud to celestial atmosphere, to win the beautiful."[39] This wonderful bit of residual symbolism is typical of
Hawthorne at his best. It is quite unobtrusive, and more or less
offhand, and is completely incapable of translation into con-
ceptual terms. The box is emblematic of Owen Warland's pursuit of the Ideal, seen in terms of light tracery in pearl on an
ebony background.

There is, I suspect, a very serious underlining here of biblical
imagery. The butterfly, of course, is a traditional symbol of
resurrection, and, at least metaphorically, the box is the chrysalis,
at once the butterfly's womb and tomb. The butterfly, when the
box is opened, flies away to return no more, and though destroyed, has spiritually ascended to God who gave it. One is
also reminded of Keats's "Ode on a Grecian Urn," the enigmatic
conclusion of which is very similar to the vision of the butterfly
ascending to heaven, pursued by the artist. Again, however, the
enigmatic nature of Truth and Beauty must be insisted on. Owen
Warland has achieved a perception of the Beautiful but has been
able to make it manifest only through a mechanical butterfly;
and ultimately, as Danforth's and Annie's comments show, this
manifestation is not understandable. If one has that knowledge
of the Beautiful which enables him to create its imperfect earthly
counterpart, then the analogy between the Ideal and the Apparent is evident. Looking at the Apparent alone, however, with

only the artist's statement that it is a copy of an Ideal, the nature of this Ideal must remain mysterious.

Hawthorne so habitually thinks in terms of the relation of the Ideal to the actual work of art that at one point he compares a woman to an artistic ideal in a pictorial image. His description of Sylph Etherege, in the story of the same name, is at once a polite compliment to a beautiful young lady, and an eloquent commentary on a mind which habitually saw art and humanity in terms of their ideal forms. "The girl's slender and sylph-like figure, tinged with radiance from the sunset clouds, and overhung with the rich drapery of the silken curtain, and set within the deep frame of the window, was a perfect picture; *or, rather, it was like the original loveliness in a painter's fancy, from which the most finished picture is but an imperfect copy* [italics mine]."[40] Sylph Etherege, in short, is almost exactly like the enigmatic model for Drowne's wooden image, who also expressed—though only to Drowne—an Ideal.

The logical extension of this idea brings us to the Castle in the Air of the Man of Fancy. In this castle is "a splendid library, the volumes of which were inestimable, because they consisted not of actual performances, but of the works which the authors only planned, without ever finding the happy season to achieve them. . . . The shelves were crowded; for it would not be too much to affirm that every author has imagined and shaped out in his thought more and far better works than those which actually proceeded from his pen."[41] The whimsicality of tone warns us not to take Hawthorne too seriously here. He seems to say that he is just playing with an idea, in a cloud-land realm where everyday reality is not to be insisted upon. Nevertheless, though whimsical in tone, the remark is evidence of an underlying concern in Hawthorne's aesthetic thought. Anyone who feels as strongly as Hawthorne does about the radical imperfection of the completed work of art when compared with the Ideal from which it came, might well solace himself by quizzically revolving the problem in his mind while safely insulated from reality in a *Chateau d'Espagne*. Only the half-crazed "P," however, the deranged author of "P's Correspondence," would ever confuse a castle in the air with reality, mixing up the two worlds of the Ideal and the Apparent. A sane man, outside of the grounds of a castle in the air, will not concern himself seriously with "the untold tales of Chaucer's Canterbury Pilgrims; the unwritten cantos of the Fairy Queen; the conclusion of Coleridge's Christabel; and the whole of Dryden's projected epic on the subject of King Arthur."[42]

One of Hawthorne's more interesting preoccupations in the problem of the relation of the artist to the Ideal lies in his probing of the question of whether or not the vision of the Ideal gives the artist in some sense a manner of control over it. Can the artist by force of his mere apprehension of Reality in some sense mold it to his will? The story of the Artist in "The Prophetic Pictures" is probably Hawthorne's most serious fictional attempt to answer this problem. The plot of this tale is an exploration of how far the Artist controls the destinies of the people whom he paints. Does the Artist who paints the pictures of Walter Ludlow and of his fiancée Elinor in some manner control their fate? Mary E. Dichmann has written a very persuasive statement that the Artist *does* control the fates of Walter and Elinor.[43] She interprets Hawthorne's view of the Artist as paradoxical. The Artist, in order to create, must be driven to the position of "a spiritualized Paul Pry."[44] The very nature of artistic creation is, she says, an adventure into the realm of the violation of a human soul. An artist, in short, must by his very artistic endeavor commit the Unpardonable Sin of violating the sanctity of a human heart. Indeed, Miss Dichmann suggests that the success of the artist may be measured by his ability to commit the Unpardonable Sin. Since the Artist of "The Prophetic Pictures" is the most successful of all the artists in Hawthorne's fiction, with the possible exception of Owen Warland, and since he depicts in these pictures the eventual catastrophe of Walter's and Elinor's marriage, it is tempting to assume that somehow the Artist himself is responsible for the tragedy. Miss Dichmann sums up her case very nicely in her statement that the story "concerns the dichotomy of the art of artistic creation, which Hawthorne seems to have felt is man's most spiritual achievement, and of that 'dark necessity', which, he feared, impels the artist by virtue of his very artistry towards the unpardonable sin, the violation of the human heart."[45]

She recognizes in the Artist an essentially Godlike perspective toward experience, that is, a view of human life in which past, present, and future have an eternal validity. She concludes that "since the power to synthesize past, present, and future gives to the artist's vision an eternal validity and to the artist an omniscience which is normally attributed only to the mind of God, it is logical to assume in the artist the ability to use his knowledge in a Godlike fashion—in other words, to create, and to comprehend the past, the present, and the future in his creation."[46] This analogy between God and the Artist is, it must be confessed, a tempting one, though ultimately, I think, false. It ignores the fact that throughout the story Hawthorne prepares the way for the eventual tragic ending. At the very beginning of the tale Walter tells Elinor that this artist "catches the secret sentiments and passions, and throws them upon the canvas, like sun-shine—or perhaps, in the portraits of dark-souled men, like a gleam of infernal fire."[47] As it turns out, the Artist does both of these things: in Elinor's portrait he depicts sunshine; in Walter's, which is truly the portrait of a dark-souled man, he catches a gleam of infernal fire. He himself, though, makes neither the celestial nor the infernal fires. He merely interprets what he, a more sensitive observer, has seen revealed in the characters of his subjects. As he says to Elinor about Walter's picture, "the artist—the true artist—must look beneath the exterior. It is his gift—his proudest, but often a melancholy one—to see the inmost soul, and, by a power indefinable even to himself, to make it glow or darken upon the canvas, in glances that express the thought and sentiment of years."[48] This does not seem to imply that the Artist is in any way creating the catastrophe which he paints. In addition, his insight has only been to put into a more concrete form what Elinor has already suspected. At the very first, when Walter has left her alone, she muses to herself, conscious of a vague premonition of evil which she is unable to define exactly. Hawthorne tells us that "when the young man had departed, it cannot be denied that a remarkable expression was again visible on the fair and youthful face of his mistress. It was a sad and anxious look, little in accordance with what should have been the feelings of a maiden on the eve of wedlock."[49] Finally, when the Artist shows her the sketch in which he has depicted Walter's eventual attempt on her life, she is able to understand the vague fear which has troubled her.[50]

The point Hawthorne is making here is, it seems, analogous to the point of "The Artist of the Beautiful." In "The Artist of the Beautiful" neither Peter Hovenden, Danforth, nor Annie can understand what Owen Warland has done, though Annie comes the closest to some conception of the artist's vision. Similarily, in "The Prophetic Pictures" there are several points of view of the character of Walter. First, and most superficial, is the judgment entirely on the basis of externals. Society's opinion of the pictures figures only very briefly in the story, when it comes to view them and decides either that they are "among the most admirable specimens of modern portraiture," or else, after comparing the portraits with the originals "feature by feature" is "rapturous in praise of the likeness."[51] Second, and somewhat more profound in her judgment, is Elinor with her vague sense of evil which she is unable to put into words. Finally, and most profound, is the vision of the Artist, who can see the inmost soul of his subject. The artistic vision, therefore, is not different in kind, but only in degree from the vision of other beings.

The Artist himself develops his attitude toward art in unambiguous terms in a soliloquy during the course of the tale.

> "O glorious Art! . . . thou art the image of the Creator's own. The innumerable forms, that wander in nothingness, start into being at thy beck. The dead live again. Thou recallest them to their old scenes, and givest their gray shadows the lustre of a better life, at once earthly and immortal. Thou snatchest back the fleeting moments of History. With thee there is no Past, for, at thy touch, all that is great becomes forever present; and illustrious men live through long ages, in the visible performance of the very deeds which made them what they are. O potent Art! as thou bringest the faintly revealed Past to stand in that

narrow strip of sunlight, which we call Now, canst thou
summon the shrouded Future to meet her there? Have I
not achieved it? Am I not thy Prophet?"[52]

The Artist's identification of himself as a "Prophet" is central
to Miss Dichmann's statement about his Godlike ability. I suspect,
rather, that Hawthorne is using the term in a more specifically
biblical sense. His artist "prophesies," i. e., "predicts" the truth
without in any sense controlling it. The biblical prophets were
able to foretell coming events only because they had been, in
some form or other, entrusted by the Deity with knowledge of
His works or plans; they did not in any sense control His
operations. And again we should notice that, although the
Artist is sure of the relation of his paintings to some ultimate
Reality, what this Reality actually *is* remains as mysterious to
us as it does to Walter and Elinor. A good analogue to the above
quotation is God's justification to the Son in *Paradise Lost,* where
He defends himself from the charge of predestining the Fall of
Adam and Eve. The whole passage is generally relevant to the
Artist's soliloquy, and God's justification of his conduct makes
the point, which Miss Dichmann overlooks, that to foreknow
something is not to *will* it to happen, but merely to have a more
profound insight into the situation. God says, as an explanation
of the role which he played in the Fall:

> They [Adam and Eve] therefore as to right belong'd,
> So were created, nor can justly accuse
> Thir maker, or thir making, or thir Fate;
> As if predestination over-rul'd
> Thir will, dispos'd by absolute Decree
> Or high foreknowledge; they themselves decreed
> Thir own revolt, not I: if I foreknew,
> Foreknowledge had no influence on their fault,
> Which had no less prov'd certain unforeknown (III, 111-19).

A second statement of Hawthorne's beliefs about the artist's
relation to the Ideal may be found in "The Birthmark." At first
glance Aylmer appears to be not an artist at all, but one of the
generally villainous crew of Hawthorne's scientists.[53] Still, I

think one might well classify Aylmer as an artist in the medium of science, if that does not confuse the issue still more. What I mean by this is that Aylmer has what one might call an artistic vision. He sees his wife Georgianna as an earthly type of a heavenly Ideal, marred only by her birthmark. Hawthorne would not, I submit, say that only the literary artist or the pictoral artist has access to the Ideal. The Ideal is common to all men, and insofar as they are capable of realizing it they are artists.

Aylmer is different from Hawthorne's other scientists, with the exception of Dr. Heidegger, in that he does not undertake his particular scientific experiments with any love for the advancement of human knowledge *as such*. Unlike Chillingworth, who uses science only as an instrument of vengeance, or Rappaccini, who at least according to his rival Baglioni, "cares infinitely more for science than for mankind," and who "would sacrifice human life, his own among the rest, or whatever else was dearest to him, for the sake of adding so much as a grain of mustard seed to the great heap of his accumulated knowledge,"[54] Aylmer "redeemed himself from materialism by his strong and eager aspiration towards the infinite"; and Georgianna reflects on his work in much the same terms that Kenyon uses to discuss his statue of Cleopatra which falls so lamentably short of the ideal: "Much as he had accomplished, she could not but observe that his most splendid successes were almost invariably failures, if compared with the ideal at which he aimed. His brightest diamonds were the merest pebbles, *and felt to be so by himself*, in comparison with the inestimable gems which lay hidden beyond his reach [italics mine]."[55] The italicized phrase emphasizes that Aylmer himself had conceived of his work in terms which Hawthorne usually reserves for descriptions of artistic endeavor. Aylmer's failure is analogous to the failure of "P" in "P's Correspondence"; neither recognizes the difference between the real and the ideal worlds. Alymer attempts to realize Ideal perfection in the world of Appearances. Unlike Kenyon, he is unwilling to admit that imperfection is a condition of this Apparent world, only to discover that the birthmark on his wife's cheek can be removed, and Georgianna made perfect, only in a world where the Ideal is not clothed in the form of the Apparent. Alymer's diamonds, which are really pebbles, serve to remind us of the reason for his failure. He has confused knowledge of Appearances with understanding of Reality, and

> Uncertain and unsettl'd still remains,
> Deep verst in books and shallow in himself,
> Crude or intoxicate, collecting toys,
> And trifles for choice matters, worth a spunge;
> As Children gathering pibles on the shore.
>
> (*Paradise Regained*, IV, 327-30)

The result of Aylmer's experiment, on the face of it, is evil. The operation was successful but the patient died. Actually, the case should be put more strongly: *because* the operation was successful—or for that matter, because it was even attempted—the patient died. Why the patient died is perfectly obvious. Aylmer was unable to separate the world of the Ideal from the world of Appearance, and had hoped to make the Ideal manifest in an imperfect world, an attempt which was, in the nature of the difference between the two worlds, doomed to failure. Somewhat the same point is made in "The Snow-Image" in a more comic vein. Here the Ideal snow-maiden is quite melted away through the well-meant but disastrous offices of Mr. Lindsey, who puts her in front of a hot stove in order to make her comfortable.

The rather obvious conclusion to "The Birthmark" may cause us to overlook Hawthorne's subsidiary statement of the unknowable nature of Reality. That Reality exists and is somehow removed from the world of flux is a basic concept in the story. Just what this Reality is, however, and how it relates to the world of Appearances is unknown both to us and to Aylmer. His artistic vision has been found wanting at the end of the tale because he lacks that "profounder wisdom" which would have realized that the world of Appearances cannot, in its very nature, contain Perfection.

Hawthorne, then, was fascinated by the relationship of the Ideal world to the Apparent, and turned again and again in his fiction to dramatization of their interdependence and interactions. In these dramatizations, however, he insists on two major points, first, that the nature of the Real world can never be known, although its existence can be posited by analogy, and second, that any attempts to classify the world of Appearances cannot be done in terms of ultimate Reality, and result not in unity but in ever greater multiplicity—in a constantly growing ambiguity of definition and multiplication of detail. Hawthorne's oft-quoted report of his final meeting with Melville forms an interesting comparison, and may incidentally serve to throw some light upon this rather perplexing literary friendship. When Melville came to see Hawthorne in Liverpool they went for an outing together, renewing the conversations they had held before when Hawthorne had lived in Lenox, and Melville only a few miles away in Pittsfield. Hawthorne, in his journal, records his impressions of the day's events:

> Melville, as he always does, began to reason of Providence and futurity, *and of everything that lies beyond human ken*, and informed me that he had "pretty much made up his mind to be annihilated;" but still he does not seem to rest in that anticipation; and, I think, will never rest until he gets hold of a definite belief. It is strange how he persists— and has persisted ever since I knew him, and probably long before—in wandering to-and-fro over these deserts, as dismal and monotonous as the sand hills amid which we were sitting. He can neither believe, nor be comfortable in his unbelief; and he is too honest and courageous not to try to do one or the other [italics mine].[56]

In addition to the italicized phrase which makes the interesting equation between Providence and futurity and all unknowable things, the whole passage represents a sympathetic statement, on Hawthorne's part, of Melville's intellectual problems, problems with which Hawthorne can sympathize and to some extent understand, but which do not really bother him. Melville's constant artistic endeavor was an attempt to grapple with the unknowable Reality that lies beneath the surface of things, an attempt to define, or at least to comprehend, the purposes of that inscrutable and ominous principle which lies behind the apparent world as we see it. Hawthorne, on the other hand, was not really interested in any such grappling with existential principles which he was willing to accept on faith and hence to dismiss as subjects of artistic concern. Since Reality was for him unknowable, he was interested in it primarily as it was shown in all its complexity in the world about him. Much less than Melville was he interested in infinite first causes; and much more in the varied interplay of incomplete and finite effects in the world as he knew it.

The Nature of Artistic Illusion

ONE OF THE more interesting ways in which Hawthorne probes the various aspects of multiplicity as an organizing aesthetic principle may be seen in his discussions of "point of view" which are found in various nonfictional and fictional contexts throughout his works. The most famous exploration of this problem, of course, appears in his definition of the Romance and the Novel in the Preface to *The House of the Seven Gables*. This Preface is the best nonfictional statement of what Hawthorne felt were two opposing ways of writing fiction, though he elaborates the basic conception in many other places as well. In effect, in this discussion of the Novel and the Romance he not only outlines the aesthetic principles which he considers fundamental to each form of art, but also admits the principle that both are valid ways of depicting Reality, each giving an insight into the world of Being. They differ from each other in their several methods of presenting this world; in the modes by which they represent it to the reader. The Novel, Hawthorne says, "is presumed to aim at a very minute fidelity, not merely to the possible, but to the probable and ordinary course of man's experience," while the Romance, though "it must rigidly subject itself to laws, and while it sins unpardonably so far as it may swerve aside from the truth of the human heart—has fairly a right to present that truth under circumstances, to a great extent, of the writer's own choosing or creation."[1]

This Preface is a theoretical defense of Hawthorne's Romantic—as he defines the Romance—art against the insensitive and misapplied canons of Realistic—or, in his phrase, Novelistic—criticism. In this Preface he pleads for serious consideration of the Romance on its own grounds, as a serious method of depicting Reality, even though the mode of expression is not Novelistic. Although the Romance has "a certain latitude, both as to its fashion and material"[2] which the Novel does not possess, this does not disqualify the Romance as a serious art form, nor, *ipso facto*, relegate it to the category of escape fiction. Both the Novel and the Romance imitate "the truth of the human heart" but in different ways, and consequently neither can be judged by standards of the other. In other words, both the Novel and the Romance, insofar as they imitate the Ideal at all, are similar. Where they differ from each other is in their method of depicting this Ideal world; and here, it may be parenthetically added, is exactly where *all* forms of art differ from one another. Hawthorne himself, as his admiration for Trollope bears ample witness, was no despiser of the Novel, although he knew that his own artistic talents did not qualify him as a novelist.

The rules by which the novelist (as opposed to the romancer) molds his art are in Hawthorne's mind roughly equatable with what we today would call standards of the "realistic" novel, as opposed to the "symbolic" novel, which is closer to what Hawthorne would call the Romance. Since the Romance has a certain latitude in fashion and material, it would seem to follow that a Romance achieves its effect by a kind of imposition of illusion *as illusion* on a reader, whereas a Novel achieves its effect by creating through illusion a sense of counterfeit reality. Consequently, the great aim of a romancer is to create a certain atmosphere or tone surrounding his work which will give the reader an intuitive glimpse of the reality he is trying to express. As Hawthorne wrote, half-ironically, to Fields, in November of 1850, "The fact is, in writing a romance, a man is always, or always ought to be, careering on the utmost verge of a precipitous absurdity, and the skill lies in coming as close as possible, without actually tumbling over."[3]

One must carefully guard against taking this statement, or any similar one, as self-deprecatory. As in this quotation, Hawthorne often writes in a humorous manner, but this does not invalidate the seriousness of his meaning. He does *not* mean, although he is often so interpreted, that the romancer deserves

good-natured contempt for having gotten into such a position
in the first place, that he should not have written the kind of art
where he is on the verge of absurdity, and that a better artist
would have avoided the whole predicament which the inferior
artist, once being in, must struggle out of as best he can.

A more expanded statement of the same line of argument may
be found in the short Preface to "Rappaccini's Daughter," where
Hawthorne, in the person of an anonymous critic, appraises the
work of one M. de l'Aubépine. This critic begins by stating Hawthorne's position which is, he decides, somewhere between that
of the Transcendentalists and that of "the great body of pen-and-
ink men who address the intellect and sympathies of the multitude." M. de l'Aubépine is "too remote, too shadowy, and unsubstantial in his modes of development to suit the taste of the latter
class, and yet too popular to satisfy the spiritual or metaphysical
requisitions of the former," a situation which necessarily finds
him without an audience, except for "here and there an individual
or possibly an isolated clique."[4]

The comic tone of this statement on the part of the anonymous
critic should be noted here. The fact that a point could be stated
comically seems to have been, if anything, a recommendation to
Hawthorne who, unlike many of his critics, was never prone to
equate seriousness of meaning with soberness of expression.
Hawthorne here uses a typical device, developing a serious point
by means of a comic mode of statement. This Preface, though
sometimes interpreted as an indication of Hawthorne's sense of
isolation from the audience he wished to address and from the
world in general, is really nothing of the kind. It is a defiant
statement of artistic purpose. Hawthorne is isolated from the
world's appreciation, he seems to say, not because of any
inability to communicate, but because what he has to say depends on his manner of saying it and neither the Transcendentalists nor the multitude particularly want to take the trouble to
listen. The implied condemnation, however, as Hawthorne develops it, is not a condemnation so much of the author as of the
audience. It is the insensitive or obstinate reader rather than the
unpopular author who is weighed in the balance and found wanting. The anonymous critic goes on to say, of Aubépine's work:

His writings, to do them justice, are not altogether des-
titute of fancy and originality; they might have won him
greater reputation but for an inveterate love of allegory,
which is apt to invest his plots and characters with the
aspect of scenery and people in the clouds, and to steal
away the human warmth out of his conceptions. . . . In
any case, he generally contents himself with a very slight
embroidery of outward manners,—the faintest possible
counterfeit of real life,—and endeavors to create an interest
by some less obvious peculiarity of the subject.[5]

Here is the whole definition of the Novel and the Romance
restated. The critic is making the point that Aubépine's audience
would prefer him to write novels, but he either cannot or (more
likely) will not. His attempts to create interest in his work by
being true to some other aspect of reality than that of "outward
manners," though it costs him more of his audience, is not, it
must be emphasized again, a literary apology. Indeed, this entire
Preface, which can be hastily interpreted as a kind of shamefaced
literary retraction, is in reality closer to a manifesto. And the
anonymous critic gives the whole argument away when he says:
"We will only add to this very cursory notice that M. de l'Aubépine's productions, *if the reader chance to take them in precisely
the proper point of view, may amuse a leisure hour as well as
those of a brighter man; if otherwise, they can hardly fail to look
excessively like nonsense* [italics mine]."[6]

Hawthorne is not begging the reader in this passage that he
be so kind as to demean himself in the attempt to take these
productions in precisely the point of view required by their
(small) merit; he is saying rather that the reader must take the
point of view required by any work of art in order to interpret
that work of art. Hawthorne felt that his art was difficult, that to
understand and enjoy it required some concentration, and that
it would discourage and disappoint those who were not willing
to accept, at least hypothetically, Hawthorne's point of view as
expressed in any given tale. He did not feel, nor does he state,
that one of the unfortunate shortcomings of his art was that
everyone could not understand it on the first cursory reading.

With such an opinion the author must be prepared to accept the fact that he will probably not be popular, if only because the conditions which he attaches to his art will discourage the casual turner of pages. And, indeed, such was Hawthorne's opinion. Although he sometimes wished for popularity, it was not on an artistic but an economic basis. Had he been a more popular author he would have been wealthier, and he knew it. Good art was, however, not necessarily popular art any more than it was necessarily unpopular. To the best of my knowledge Hawthorne never made either of the easy equations—that of the successful writer that popularity equals quality, or that of the unsuccessful one that popularity equals superficiality. Hawthorne does not really think in these terms, although at times his professional jealousy can cause him to inveigh against particular literary dislikes, notably women writers, with considerable vehemence. Trollope was a very popular writer and Hawthorne envied him none of his popularity; nor, on the other hand, was Hawthorne swept away by the acclaim which greeted each new best-seller. He is very clear in his position that popularity does not of itself have any relation to literary merit, especially in one letter to Lewis Mansfield, a minor poet who had submitted his poem "The Morning Watch" to Hawthorne for criticism. He replied to Mansfield, who was apparently worried that his poem was too personal, in unambiguous terms:

> Your poem is addressed not to the world at large, but to a class of cognate minds—to those most capable of understanding you—to your purest and closest friends, wherever they may be scattered throughout the world, who will never know you save through this work, but will nevertheless know you better than most of those who are familiar with your face. To whom should you speak of matters near your heart, if not to these invisible friends? You need not dread being overheard, however loudly you may speak. Your voice—or, at least, your meaning—will reach only those who are privileged to hear and understand it, and what sense is there in caring one fig about the helter-skelter judgments of those who cannot understand you. It might be, that only one person in the whole world would understand,

while all the rest would ridicule you; but it would be worth a life's labor to be understood by that one, while the ridicule of the others would not be worth a thought.[7]

In one sense this letter is only a rather conventional statement of the bounds of propriety to a young man who feels somewhat trapped within the genteel tradition; on the other hand, the statement is a profoundly serious one in its implications. What Hawthorne is affirming is the austere doctrine that the audience must stoop to art, not art to the audience. If a work is good—and for the purposes of this discussion it is not really germane to examine Hawthorne's opinions about the merits of Lewis Mansfield's poetry—the audience must come to it. The "class of cognate minds" may be small, may indeed be only one person, but this really makes no difference. Indeed, Hawthorne does not feel that a work's popularity forms any reliable guide at all to its value.

Hawthorne constantly reiterates his belief that a work of art which is in any way Romantic in form achieves its effect through a certain mood which it induces into the reader, a mood which is in no way equatable with vagueness. Imprecision for some precise effect, although probably ultimately a paradox, seems to be pretty near Hawthorne's own view. He writes Lewis Mansfield, apparently in reply to some query about whether or not the story of "The Morning Watch" was too vague, a very polite answer saying that it certainly was. He justifies his remarks on vagueness in the following way: "In a story like this, it is allowable, and highly advisable, (as you yourself have felt) to have as much mist and glorified fog as possible, diffused about on all sides, but still there should be a distinct pathway to tread upon—a clue that the reader shall confide in, as being firmly fixed somewhere."[8] The mist, in other words, is not gratuitous, nor put in for purposes of confusion but rather for purposes of clarification. The glorified fog should not obscure the pathway but should somehow set it off by contrast or by adding implications to the overt meaning. Fog in itself is just confusion, and confusion is not art. The mist should be used for a definite purpose, glorified with meaning, and in Hawthorne's own practice this glorification consists in multiplying the various possibilities of interpretation which arise out of any single action.

Hawthorne's artistic belief that Romantic art must attempt to induce a certain mood into the reader may be seen in other Prefaces than that to *The House of the Seven Gables,* though not stated so didactically. The Preface to *Twice-Told Tales,* which is chiefly quoted today because it contains the loaded statement that the Tales "have the pale tint of flowers that blossomed in too retired a shade," is a case in point. Hawthorne, in this Preface, begins by telling why the tales were never very popular; indeed, he even wonders how they ever attained the little popularity they actually did manage to achieve. He assigns several reasons for their failure to attract a wide audience: they are too meditative, too allegorical, sentimental instead of passionate, and generally too tame. Hawthorne closes this list of faults with a defensive statement. "The book," he says "if you would see anything in it, requires to be read in the clear, brown, twilight atmosphere in which it was written; if opened in the sunshine, it is apt to look exceedingly like a volume of blank pages."[9] Again I would insist that this is not an apologetic statement about the quality of the tales themselves. The tales are forgotten because people will not take the trouble to read them; though Hawthorne denies that they are vague. "Every sentence . . . may be understood and felt by anybody who will give himself the trouble to read it, and will take up the book in a proper mood."[10]

Here is the crux of whole matter. Few people are willing to take up such an apparently unpromising book in the mood which it requires. This is not, Hawthorne says, in any way the fault of the book, nor are the tales to be blamed for the reader's unwillingness to bother with them. Stories of the type of the *Twice-Told Tales* cannot reasonably expect a large audience, nor, Hawthorne suggests, is a large audience per se particularly desirable, repeating his earlier statement to Lewis Mansfield. Again, however, the fault is the reader's, not the author's. The reader, in order to interpret the tales, must come to them; the author cannot condescend to make things easier, for what he has to say depends completely on his manner of saying it.

Hawthorne again gives expression to this idea that the audience must take the validity of an artistic mood on faith in his sketch "Main Street." In this rather incidental work a "respectable-looking" individual using a "pictorial exhibition"[11] delivers a popularized history of Salem. After enticing his audience into a room before a mysterious curtain, the impresario treats them to a history of the Main Street of Salem, replete with moralizations and more or less appropriate historic comments. The story is attached to a recognizable everyday context only through the person of the showman who, before the story is very far advanced, has gotten involved in an argument with one of his patrons. This running quarrel between the "artist" and the "audience" serves primarily to give comic relief to what is basically a rather feeble story, but the comedy makes a serious point. The long quarrel, which is eventually resolved only by refunding the patron's money, deals with the theme I have explored above, the quality of the "illusion" which art presents.

The showman begins his spiel with a facile explanation of what he is going to do, and a promise of good entertainment, "unless something should go wrong," such as the misplacing of a picture, "whereby the people and events of one century might be thrust into the middle of another," thus breaking one of the few laws to which such a show should conform, or "the breaking of a wire, which would bring the course of time to a sudden period."[12]

The entertainment begins with a description of the early town in the time of the Indians, during the reign of the Squaw Sachem and her husband, the magician Wappacowet. At the conclusion of the showman's somewhat slick commentary, however, "an acidulous-looking gentleman in blue glasses" speaks up acrimoniously: "The whole affair is a manifest catchpenny!" he says, and goes on to explain why. "The trees look more like weeds in a garden than a primitive forest; the Squaw Sachem and Wappacowet are stiff in their pasteboard joints; and the squirrels, the deer, and the wolf move with all the grace of a child's wooden monkey, sliding up and down a stick." The showman is really unable to reply, but he suggests a possible remedy to the defects of the performance. "Human art has its limits," he says, "and we must now and then ask a little aid from the spectator's imagination." This aid the gentleman has no intention of giving.

As will become only too clear in the course of the story, what the gentleman really expects is for the showman's exhibition to conform to laws which are not its own, indeed, to laws of strict realism. He prefers to see things "precisely as they are."[13] What the gentleman is really asking, in terms of Hawthorne's dichotomy between the Novel and the Romance, is that a Romantic production such as this conform to his Novelistic preconceptions of art. Hawthorne, although he admits that the showman's exhibition may leave something to be desired as a form of aesthetic expression, has no sympathy for the captious criticism of the spectacled observer. Later on in the story the point is again brought home. The showman has introduced as a model of ideal beauty Anna Gower, Governor Endicott's first wife. The gentleman finds this "too ridiculous!—positively insufferable!" He is able to see only a "pasteboard figure, such as a child would cut out of a card, with a pair of very dull scissors," and the showman is unable to convince him of his error, even by suggesting significantly that he change his seat to get a different perspective. The gentleman will have none of such subterfuges, replying again that it is his business "to see things just as they are."[14] By this time the refrain has taken on a very definite ironic flavor. We are becoming only too conscious that the gentleman, by seeing things just as they are, is in reality seeing nothing at all. Things, as we realize although the critic does not, are not in their nature knowable "just as they are."

Once again, after allowing the show to continue for a few moments, the critic breaks in. The showman gets as far as the times of Governor Winthrop, when he is again interrupted by another critic who objects to certain genealogical irregularities in the arrangement of the historical figures. This critic, who is a man of some faith in the artistic method, is joined by the spectacled gentleman who gives the final word on the quality of the "illusion": "Illusion! What illusion? . . . On the word of a gentleman, I see nothing illusive in the wretchedly bedaubed sheet of canvas that forms your background, or in these paste-

board slips that hitch and jerk along the front." The showman
suggests once more that he change his seat for a better perspective; and again the critic refuses.[15] So the story continues,
with the critic occasionally interrupting, though always refusing
to leave, or, until the very end, to take back his money. Captain
Gardner, the hero of the battle of Bloody Brook in King Philip's
War, rides a steed, which according to the critic, "looks like a
pig"; indeed, Captain Gardner himself looks like the devil,
though, the gentleman sarcastically adds, "a very tame one, and
on a most diminutive scale." Finally, at the end of the exhibition,
his money is refunded and he leaves, muttering that the entertainment was a "humbug."[16]

To leave the exhibition with the point of view of the critic
is, nevertheless, to misunderstand the whole series of exchanges
between him and the showman. The showman has attempted to
make the raw materials of history into a work of art, and Hawthorne suggests by the incident of the breaking wire that this
particular work of art may not be too good a one. But the critic
has not come to any realization of why the work of art is no
good, if indeed this is the case; he only knows that he will not be
fooled by any illusions. The showman suggests that *any* art
requires illusion to produce the effect of truth, and that the
quality of the truth expressed is dependent on the acceptance of
the truth of this illusion. The critic, however, refuses to admit
this. Truth is truth, and illusion is illusion, and he prefers to see
things just as they are.

Hawthorne stated the relation of illusion to truth quite suc-
cinctly in another incidental sketch, "Sunday at Home." At one
point he engages in speculating whether Sabbath sunshine is
holier and brighter than that of weekdays. He concludes that,
though this cannot be proven, still "many have fancied so"
and, even though not capable of scientific demonstration, still,
"some illusions, and this among them, are the *shadows* of great
truths [italics mine]."[17]

Often Hawthorne's Prefaces show this same concern with the
quality of the illusion which will be shown in the Romance to
follow. The Preface to *The Scarlet Letter*, the often discussed
"Custom House" essay, forms only an apparent exception. This

essay was supposedly written to give brightness to what Hawthorne felt was too grim a tale to sell without some sort of popular
essay prefixed to it; and of course, as everyone knows, *The
Scarlet Letter* was originally planned as one of a collection of
several short stories to be included in a volume entitled "Old-
Time Legends: Together with Sketches, Experimental and
Ideal."[18] Recently, though, Charles Feidelson has suggested a
more integral relation of the "Custom House" to *The Scarlet
Letter* proper. He has attempted to show that both the worlds of
the Custom House and of seventeenth-century New England are
symbolically linked together through the symbol of The Scarlet
Letter, which is a symbol of a mode of perception as well as an
emblem for adultery:

> In this way "The Custom House" throws light on a theme
> in *The Scarlet Letter* which is easily overlooked amid the
> ethical concerns of the book. Every character, in effect,
> re-enacts the "Custom House" scene in which Hawthorne
> himself contemplated the letter, so that the entire "romance"
> becomes a kind of exposition of the nature of symbolic
> perception. Hawthorne's subject is not only the meaning
> of adultery but also meaning in general; not only what the
> focal symbol means but also how it gains significance.[19]

As Feidelson sees the essay, then, the "Custom House" forms
an analogue to *The Scarlet Letter* by being a separate mode of
perceiving the common reality represented symbolically by the
letter itself. One might expand this idea, though with some
caution, into a kind of analogue of the difference between the
Novel and the Romance. If anything, the essay is a kind of Novel
in miniature, a *novella* if you will. One can very easily imagine
Stephen Crane writing about the "Scarlet Letter" in terms of
the Custom House and, indeed, his own "red badge of courage"
is not too disparate a symbol. In this hypothetical novel the content of the symbol would be developed through intimations of
the various ways in which the Custom House employees and
visitors do not understand its meaning, and the novel would
achieve its effect by a statement of negative ironies.

One might take, as a purely hypothetical example, Crane's

Maggie, who both in her crime against society and in society's revenge against her forms a very good foil to Hester Prynne. Maggie's tragedy, or whatever it is, is shown in the story "Maggie" through Crane's description of a series of incidents which lead to her "fall" and eventual death. The poignancy of the story depends to a large extent on the fact that we as readers have an insight into Maggie's character which the other characters in the tale do not. This ironic content of the tale is shown again and again in scenes where we can see that Maggie is being used or misunderstood or handled in an inhuman and cruel manner in the name of decency and morality. The story is an exercise in the ironic mode, conceived in terms of negatives.

The same thing is true of "The Custom House" where the only character—Hawthorne—who is capable of a positive insight into the meaning of the Scarlet Letter is rendered impotent except as a gatherer of historical data. The denizens of the Custom House would have no more insight into the meaning of the "fall" of Hester Prynne than the Bowery characters had into the analogous "fall" of Maggie. Nevertheless, I think Hawthorne intimates by his use of the Custom House sketch that the insight of the various habitués of the Salem wharves would be a valid vehicle for artistic expression of the story of the Scarlet Letter, even though he himself would not be capable of writing it. The writing of a full-length study of the Scarlet Letter in terms of the Custom House would have to be attempted by Stephen Crane, as I have suggested, or Trollope, as Hawthorne would suggest. Nevertheless, the story could be written in these terms, and would be as valid in its perception into reality as is the Romance of *The Scarlet Letter* as Hawthorne wrote it, though its method of presentation would be very different.

Hawthorne reflects in "The Custom House" that its arbitrary divorce from *The Scarlet Letter* was perhaps not wholly fortunate, as if to express the validity of the claims of the Novel to represent serious symbolic art.

> The wiser effort would have been to diffuse thought and imagination through the opaque substance of to-day, and thus to make it a bright transparency; to spiritualize the

burden that began to weigh so heavily; to seek, resolutely, the true and indestructible value that lay hidden in the petty and wearisome incidents, and ordinary characters, with which I was now conversant. The fault was mine. The page of life that was spread out before me seemed dull and commonplace, only because I had not fathomed its deeper import. A better book than I shall ever write was there; leaf after leaf presenting itself to me, just as it was written out by the reality of the flitting hour, and vanishing as fast as written, only because my brain wanted the insight and my hand the cunning to transcribe it. At some future day, it may be, I shall remember a few scattered fragments and broken paragraphs, and write them down, and find the letters turn to gold upon the page.[20]

What Hawthorne suggests here is that the best form of art, if such a form were possible, would combine the Novel with the Romance, would blend both methods of depicting Reality into one. The picture—which Hawthorne admits that he could not draw—would have been more complete had it united the Novelistic mode of perception with the Romantic,[21] had it enabled us to see the enigmatic symbol of the Scarlet Letter from two completely distinct and apparently irreconcilable points of view.

Less theoretical and perhaps more valuable comment on the illusion of reality given in the Romance may be gleaned from the Preface to *The Marble Faun*. Despite the guide-book aspects of this work, Hawthorne specifically disclaimed any intention of writing a book *about* Italy, at least any more than incidentally. He proposed merely to write "a fanciful story, evolving a thoughtful moral," not "a portraiture of Italian manners and character," for "he has lived too long abroad not to be aware that a foreigner seldom acquires that knowledge of a country at once flexible and profound, which may justify him in endeavoring to idealize its traits." Yet the choice of Italy as a background was not accidental; Hawthorne chose Italy as the scene of the Romance because it afforded him "a sort of poetic or fairy precinct, where actualities would not be so terribly insisted upon as they are . . . in America." In other words, Hawthorne saw in Italy a symbolic background where he could write in a purely Romantic mode, without worrying unduly about inducing the reader to a perception of it. "No author," he continues, "without a trial, can conceive of the difficulty of writing a romance about a country where there is no shadow, no antiquity, no mystery, no picturesque and gloomy wrong, nor anything but a commonplace prosperity. . . . Romance and poetry, ivy, lichens, and wall-flowers, need ruin to make them grow."[22]

Most readers of *The Marble Faun* have felt that Hawthorne made an error in judgment, that the Italian medium would not take care of itself when left alone, but needed to be just as thoroughly developed as the "broad and simple daylight" of America in order to have any symbolic background meaning or to induce any mood of Romance into the reader. Roy Harvey Pearce, in a very fine discussion of *The Marble Faun,* has attempted to explain the failure of the Romance totally in terms of Hawthorne's lack of comprehension of the meaning of his Italian experience.[23] Hawthorne, so this general line of argument runs, relied too heavily upon the Italian background to carry its own meaning, without realizing that this meaning was not self-evident to any eyes but his own. His description of what he hoped to attain by the use of an Italian background is an implicit statement of what he assumed everyone felt when in Rome. But not all people, and certainly not those who have never been to the Eternal City, see the same complex of meaning in the symbol "Rome" as Hawthorne does. "Rome" in itself is just as enigmatic a symbol as "The Scarlet Letter," and Hawthorne made a great error in judgment in not realizing this.

Actually, this argument is not so open and shut as it at first appears. *The Marble Faun* is a greater novel than most critics are inclined to admit, and recent scholarship has just begun to show the complex and sophisticated symbolic substructure to it. It is almost as if, with this novel, for the first time Hawthorne found what he had feared of the *Twice-Told Tales*—that his audience had dwindled to an isolated clique or a few individuals.

The complaints which Hawthorne received about *The Marble Faun's* vagueness caused him to write a final closing section for the second edition. In this explanation he really explains nothing at all, but contents himself with redefining his artistic concerns.

He takes cognizance of only one criticism of the book, that in some way its "mood"—its Roman atmosphere—had proved too unsubstantial for most of his audience. He is rather bitter about this failure in perception, but not bitter toward himself so much as *toward his readers*. He is reluctant to explain the meaning of the obscure parts of the Romance, he says, "because the necessity makes him sensible that he can have succeeded but imperfectly, at best, in throwing about this Romance the kind of atmosphere essential to the effect at which he aimed."

> He designed the story and the characters to bear, of course, a certain relation to human nature and human life, but still to be so artfully and airily removed from our mundane sphere, that some laws and proprieties of their own should be implicitly and insensibly acknowledged.
> The idea of the modern Faun, for example, loses all the poetry and beauty which the Author fancied in it, and becomes nothing better than a grotesque absurdity, if we bring it into the actual light of day. He had hoped to mystify this anomalous creature between the Real and the Fantastic, in such a manner that the reader's sympathies might be excited to a certain pleasurable degree, without impelling him to ask how Cuvier would have classified poor Donatello, or to insist upon being told, in so many words, whether he had furry ears or no. As respects all who ask such questions, the book is, to that extent, a failure.[24]

I think it need only be pointed out here that Hawthorne is again insisting upon the difference between Novelistic and Romantic standards in art. Romantic standards depend upon an artistic removal from the canons of realism to a realm where they may have laws and proprieties which belong to themselves. The failure of the book, as Hawthorne sees it, lies in the fact that he has been unable, apparently, to recreate this realm in a satisfactory manner. Hawthorne had hoped to create a mood in which the question of whether or not the Faun had hairy ears would be irrelevant to any discussion of the book, not an atmosphere in which the Faun's ears would be the subject of passionate inquiry. We must be on guard, however, in assum-

ing that Hawthorne's statement represents an unqualified admission of the book's artistic failure. Some evidence that this was
not his view at all appears in a letter he wrote to William D.
Ticknor on April 6, 1860, about the book's reception: "I have
been much gratified by the kind feeling and generous praise
contained in the notices you sent me . . . But in fact, if I have
written anything well, it should be this Romance; for I have
never thought or felt more deeply, or taken more pains."[25] And
he himself never publicly admitted that the novel was in any
way a disappointment.

The whole apparent apology in the Conclusion to the second
edition bears a remarkable similarity to the showman's remarks
to the bespectacled gentleman in "Main Street." Hawthorne does
not say that the book is in any way a failure to anyone except
those who insist on being told "in so many words" whether or
not Donatello had furry ears. He does *not* mean that anyone
who reads the book must inevitably ask this question, and the
assumption seems to be that intelligent readers will not. The
opprobrium, if there is any, is again cast on the insensitivity of
the reader rather than on the incompetence of the author.

Hawthorne's A *Wonder-Book* gives another expression to his
views on the nature of artistic illusion. The book consists of
a series of classical myths retold for children. To hold the interest of young readers, Hawthorne invents a framework for the
myths themselves, which consists of a rather ephemeral plot
about one Eustace Bright, a young college man, who tells the
tales to a group of children at "Tanglewood." In order to keep the
framework from deteriorating into mechanical repetition of a
set formula wherein Eustace Bright simply tells a story, Hawthorne has Bright tell the myths in various places about Tanglewood, and has the children comment upon the stories as they
are told. The device is basically the same as the debate between
the showman and his critic in "Main Street." Bright has told
but two myths, however, when among his youthful auditors
appears a young man who bears a rather frightening resemblance
to the bespectacled gentleman heckler in that story. This little
fellow is named "Sweet Fern" and is, Hawthorne somewhat
ironically says, "a good little boy, who was always making

particular inquiries about the precise height of giants and the littleness of fairies." After Bright has told the story of King Midas and the Golden Touch, into which he has interpolated an apocryphal episode about King Midas' daughter Marygold, whom Midas has turned to gold along with everything else, Sweet Fern solemnly asks: "How big was Marygold, and how much did she weigh after she was turned to gold?" Eustace replies: "She was about as tall as you are, . . . and, as gold is very heavy, she weighed at least two thousand pounds, and might have been coined into thirty or forty thousand gold dollars."[26] For the moment, Hawthorne leaves Sweet Fern to enjoy this metallurgical information, but the stage has been set for his eventual come-uppance. Hawthorne's whole implied meaning here, in this humorous bit of dialogue, is that Sweet Fern has made just the same mistake as have the scientific readers of *The Marble Faun* or the bespectacled critic in "Main Street." He has not understood the story because he has not attempted to understand it in the correct mood. The meaning of the tale has nothing to do with how much Marygold weighed, and her value to Midas was not, let us say, forty thousand dollars and seventy-five cents, but rather a quantity which was not measurable in gold coin.

Sweet Fern, however, has not learned his lesson. After Eustace Bright tells his next tale, the story of Pandora's Box, the following conversation takes place:

> "Cousin Eustace," said Sweet Fern, "did the box hold all the trouble that has ever come into the world?"
> "Every mite of it!" answered Eustace. . . .
> "And how big was the box?" asked Sweet Fern.
> "Why, perhaps three feet long," said Eustace, "two feet wide, and two feet and a half high."
> "Ah," said the child, "you are making fun of me, Cousin Eustace! I know there is not trouble enough in the world to fill such a great box as that. . . ."[27]

The irony could not be nicer. With all his scientific rationalism and concern for facts, Sweet Fern has come up with just exactly the wrong conclusion. With all his concern for nothing but the facts he is completely incapable of understanding their significance, and triumphantly demolishes the story on the basis of what Hawthorne at least would consider to be a complete misunderstanding of the circumstances. The only thing which saves Sweet Fern is that he, like the bespectacled critic, does not know what he is missing. He may not appreciate the beauties of the myths, but he is not troubled by any disquieting belief that there may be some meaning in these tales which escapes him.

After the next story, which is Hawthorne's version of Hercules' quest for the three Golden Apples of the Garden of the Hesperides, Sweet Fern again makes the malappropriate comment. The discussion centers on the giant, Atlas:

> "Cousin Eustace," demanded Sweet Fern, who had been sitting at the story-teller's feet, with his mouth wide open, "exactly how tall was this giant?"
>
> "O Sweet Fern, Sweet Fern!" cried the student, "do you think I was there, to measure him with a yard-stick? Well, if you must know to a hair's-breadth, I suppose he might be from three to fifteen miles straight upward, and that he might have seated himself on Taconic, and had Monument Mountain for a footstool."
>
> "Dear me!" ejaculated the good little boy, with a contented sort of a grunt, "that was a giant, sure enough! And how long was his little finger?"
>
> "As long as from Tanglewood to the lake," said Eustace.
>
> "Sure enough, that was a giant!" repeated Sweet Fern, in an ecstasy at the precision of these measurements. . . ."[28]

Sweet Fern wants to know *exactly* how tall the giant was; no approximate answer will do. When Eustace Bright attempts to reason with him, and to suggest that perhaps the question is really irrelevant, Sweet Fern is completely unimpressed. All he has learned from the tale of the Golden Apples of the Hesperides is the approximate size of a giant, and even this bit of information came from a man who was not quite sure of his facts.

Perhaps Sweet Fern is not alone to blame for his misunderstanding of the story, however, since he comes from a family with a classical background which insists upon high standards of scholarly decorum and textual excellence. Eustace Bright has

told the story of the Golden Apples of the Hesperides not only to
the children but to their guardian, a classicist with the rather
chilling name of Pringle. Mr. Pringle, like Sweet Fern, can see
nothing worth while in Eustace Bright's reworking of the myths.
In fact, he is much more openly critical than little Sweet Fern,
and quite sweeping in his condemnation:

> "I find it impossible to express such an opinion of this story
> [he begins] as will be likely to gratify, in the smallest
> degree, your pride of authorship. Pray let me advise you
> never more to meddle with a classical myth. Your imagina-
> tion is altogether Gothic, and will inevitably Gothicize
> everything that you touch. The effect is like bedaubing a
> marble statue with paint. This giant, now! How can you
> have ventured to thrust his huge, disproportioned mass
> among the seemly outlines of Grecian fable, the tendency
> of which is to reduce even the extravagant within limits,
> by its pervading elegance?"[29]

It is not, I suspect, entirely accidental that both critics of
Eustace Bright seize upon his representation of the giant, an
aspect of the story which is quite beside its real point, as the
most worthy of comment. The apparent difference between their
two criticisms should not disguise the fact that they are basically
the same in that they do not take into account the author's attempt to create a certain mood in his audience. Sweet Fern is
so captivated with the "facts" of the case that he is unable to
look beyond them to see what they mean, while Mr. Pringle is
unwilling to admit that any mode of expression is proper to art
except that which lies within the rather narrow limits of an
elegant classicism. Eustace Bright's answer to Mr. Pringle's
criticism is an expanded version of his reproach to Sweet Fern.
Mr. Pringle, Eustace suggests, has not put himself in the proper
mood to appreciate the story. Eustace says:

> "I described the giant as he appeared to me. . . . And,
> sir, if you would only bring your mind into such a relation
> with these fables as is necessary in order to remodel them,
> you would see at once that an old Greek had no more exclu-
> sive right to them than a modern Yankee has. They are the

common property of the world, and of all time. . . . My own opinion is, that the Greeks, by taking possession of these legends (which were the immemorial birthright of mankind), and putting them into shapes of indestructible beauty, indeed, but cold and heartless, have done all subsequent ages an incalculable injury."[30]

It is always dangerous to equate the views of a character in a work of fiction with those of his author. Still, Eustace's manifesto here is almost identical with Hawthorne's own statement to Fields in regard to his purpose in "Gothicizing" the myths. "I mean to write, within six weeks or two months next ensuing, a book of stories made up of classical myths. . . . Unless I greatly mistake, these old fictions will work up admirably for the purpose [of writing a suitable book for children]; and I shall aim at substituting a tone in some degree Gothic or romantic, or any such tone as may best please myself, instead of the classic coldness, which is as repellent as the touch of marble."[31]

This final example has once more emphasized Hawthorne's artistic belief that the mood of a Romance is of the utmost importance. Any work of art depends partially for its effect on the creation of illusion; the Novel, in Hawthorne's terms, makes an illusion of life; the Romance, conversely, uses illusion *as illusion* to give a perception of some kind of Reality which is true, but not true to the laws of realistic presentation. To understand such an illusion the reader must be prepared to surrender his beliefs in the natural world of cause and effect for the obviously unreal world of Romance. In other words, the appreciation of Romance as an art form depends upon the reader's ability to recognize the validity of at least two forms of artistic representation—the realistic and the symbolic. Where the insensitive critics—Sweet Fern, Mr. Pringle, and the bespectacled gentleman—fail is in their inability to admit more than one possible way to express an unknowable Reality. They admit the validity of the Novel because they do not understand that it, like the Romance, is essentially an illusory mode of presenting Reality. In each case the illusion presented is emblematic of a higher and ultimately unknowable Reality. In the sense that all art is illusion, the Romance and the Novel are the same; where they differ from one another is in their individual kinds of illusion, the Novel giving an illusion of external appearances while the Romance insists on the validity of illusion in and for itself. To understand the meaning of a Romance the reader must have some perception of the unreal atmosphere of the tale, and must realize that illusion is, in a larger sense, truth. The artist, by various means, attempts to induce this mood into the reader's mind, independently of the Novelistic laws of fidelity to the details of external life. If the reader, however, refuses to be persuaded, the author can really do nothing about it. Responsiveness to a work of art is in a large measure the reader's responsibility and although the artist may attempt to persuade him he can never beguile him absolutely against his will. The reader must at least be willing to accept the artistic validity of the world of illusion.

III

Hawthorne's "Allegory"

PROBABLY no aspect of Hawthorne's art has been so widely discussed as has been his use of "allegory." Critics have generally used this term in a faintly pejorative sense, carrying the implication that Hawthorne, though he wrote allegory consciously, was too great an artist to be confined by it. When he is at his best, the argument runs, he transcends himself, and his allegory becomes something else. As R. H. Fogle notes: " 'Hawthorne,' his critics say in effect, 'was an inveterate allegorist. Allegory is an inferior kind of art. Hawthorne was, however, indubitably a great writer.' And there the matter rests, with the implication that Hawthorne might have been greater still if he had chosen a different mode of expression. This implication may be correct; if he had been able to apply his genius otherwise than he did, who knows what results might have been achieved? But the speculation is a trifle barren."[1] Actually, Hawthorne's critics have not by any means been generally so charitable. W. C. Brownell, for example, flatly says that "a great deal of Hawthorne would be the better for the extraction of the allegorical and symbolic elements combined with it," and takes definite issue with the modern idea that Hawthorne's allegory is a kind of imperfect symbolism which improves as it becomes less tied to the specific equations of allegory. Not so, says Brownell: "Oftenest his intrusion of symbolism, that parasite on allegory itself, is a crying abuse of a perfectly superficial and trivial expedient. He was, in fact, allegory-mad."[2]

Most critics have attempted to show, however, that Hawthorne's allegory tends toward symbolism, that his allegorical types are really not so much allegories as symbolic statements. R. H. Fogle says that Hawthorne's allegory is organic to his

artistry, "an innate quality of his vision," which is "his disposition
to find spiritual meaning in all things natural and human." He
concludes that for Hawthorne "allegory is inseparable from
moral complexity and aesthetic design, qualities to be enjoyed
in themselves."[3] Charles Feidelson has stated the case against
allegory nicely, remarking that "the symbolistic and the allegorical
patterns in Hawthorne's books reach quite different conclusions,"
the symbolistic pattern leading "to an inconclusive luxuriance of
meaning," while the allegorical "imposes the pat moral and the
simplified character."[4] As the title of Feidelson's book would
indicate, he weighs his analysis in favor of the symbolistic patterns.

The over-all tendency of modern criticism has been to accord
generally with Feidelson's point, in that it has inclined to dismiss
the "allegory" in Hawthorne while praising the "symbolism."
Roy Harvey Pearce has suggested that in Hawthorne's best tales
"general operative truth [is] located immediately in the symbol,
in a character's symbolic situation, growing out of a kind of
milieu in which the symbol would have real existence";[5] and
Norman Holmes Pearson has compared Hawthorne's use of
symbols to Wagner's use of *leitmotif*, "to recall what has come
before, and to bring the mind a greater consciousness than the
ear alone can comprehend."[6] R. H. Fogle sees Hawthorne's
symbols as always tending away from allegory toward the concrete. He points out that, even in one of Hawthorne's most
"allegorical" tales, "The Minister's Black Veil," the veil "is truly
a veil, as well as an emblem of secret sin," and that the same is
true of Hawthorne's other "allegories," which he sees as somehow
super-allegorical. In accord with this general position, Fogle
sees Hawthorne's symbols as "broadly traditional, drawn from
the main stream of Western thought," and claims as well that
allegory and symbolism in Hawthorne cannot be separated except
logically for purposes of discussion. They operate at the same
time and are "organically united," with allegory being "incomplete without the addition of symbol."[7]

Basic to all these discussions is a certain implicit confusion in
the definition of the term "allegory" as applied to Hawthorne's
art, a confusion of which critics are more or less uneasily aware.

We like to define allegory in some such manner as, say, a type of art in which fictional characters are equated with abstract moral qualities. The hitch in this linking of the allegorical character with the moral trait comes in the word "equated," which implies a one-for-one definition of the two. Though this is a fine definition and undoubtedly correct in an abstract sense, nevertheless, as we actually use the term, allegory means something quite different. As we apply the term allegory to everyday concepts—or to all literary criticism which does not deal primarily in terminology—it becomes indistinguishable from the term symbolism, except in the connotation that it is somehow inferior.

This confusion in the use of the term can be nicely seen in H. H. Waggoner's definition of Hawthorne's tales as existing "in a realm somewhere between symbolism and allegory, as those terms are used today."[8] This may be very true, but the difficulty comes in deciding just how these terms really are used. I suggest that the terms are not used at all in an easily separable manner, but more or less indistinguishably, and that this confusion over the two terms has led to a great deal of speculation which has more to do with terms than with things.

Analyses of Hawthorne's art in terms of allegory have tended to become more and more complex, to show that allegory to Hawthorne meant a very different thing from what it means to us, that is, assuming for a moment that Hawthorne used the term with some symbolic reference. Darrel Abel, for instance, in what we might loosely call an "allegorical" interpretation of *The Marble Faun*, sees Hawthorne as using three kinds of characterization, though often the types are combined within a single character. He calls these three types of characters *persons*, who represent individual humanity; *types*, who represent categories of humanity; and *symbols*, who represent "simplified and intensified embodiments of distinct human traits or complexes of traits." The last two of these categories are certainly close enough together to cause some trouble in differentiation between them, and the whole problem is made more difficult by Hawthorne's trick of rolling up all three kinds of characterization into one fictional character. In addition, although Hawthorne's "symbolic" (in the sense in which Abel has previously defined the term) characters "are somewhat like the characters of a medieval morality play, each being not primarily a complex, unique, and 'real' person, but an embodiment of a possible human trait," by which he seems to mean that they approach the strictest definition of allegorical characters, nevertheless Hawthorne, "in order . . . to make his characters less general, flat, and pallid than the characters of a morality, . . . endows them with enough distinctness and accidentality to make them appear possible and actual human beings."[9]

Perhaps it would be just as well to state at once that the confusion in the term allegory stems directly from Hawthorne himself. Again and again he describes his work as "allegorical" in some way or other, though to the best of my knowledge he never uses the term "symbolic" or "symbolistic."[10] In the Preface to "Rappaccini's Daughter," Hawthorne says that his works might have been more popular except for "an inveterate love of allegory" (see above, p. 53). The two stories, "Egotism; or, the Bosom Serpent" and "The Christmas Banquet" were originally intended to be published as part of a story collection entitled "Allegories of the Heart,"[11] though the latter of these, at least, bears very little resemblance to what we would call an allegory. The best statement of what Hawthorne means by an "allegory," however, may be seen in the apparently innocent Preface to a rather early tale, "The Threefold Destiny." He says of the tale that "rather than a story of events claiming to be real, it may be considered *as an allegory,* such as the writers of the last century would have expressed in the shape of an Eastern tale, *but to which I have endeavored to give a more life-like warmth than could be infused into those fanciful productions* [italics mine]."[12]

The above definition of allegory is interesting in two ways. First of all is Hawthorne's equation of his "allegory" with "a more life-like warmth" than that found in the Eastern tale, although we would be inclined to define "allegory" as giving, if anything, a *less* life-like warmth. Whether or not Hawthorne was successful in giving this warmth to the tale is beside the point; significant for our purposes is only that he felt that allegory was not necessarily a form of art which led to coldness and abstraction.

The second interesting feature of this definition lies in Hawthorne's equation of this story with the Eastern tale. He says, in effect, that this tale is an allegory *as were* the Eastern tales of the eighteenth century.

The definition of the Eastern tale as allegorical is worth a brief note. It is impossible to discover at this late date just what tales Hawthorne had in mind when he lumped them all together as "Eastern tales." The Eastern tale underwent a considerable vogue in those late eighteenth-century periodicals with which Hawthorne was fairly well acquainted, and he also knew some other Oriental tales.[13] Two other Eastern tales which he certainly knew were Beckford's *Vathek* and Dr. Johnson's *Rasselas*. The first of these has no significance for "The Threefold Destiny," though the punishment of sinners in the Halls of Eblis may have suggested Dimmesdale's burning heart in *The Scarlet Letter*[14]; but the second forms an interesting parallel.

The story of "The Threefold Destiny" is a rather pat little moralizing legend about one Ralph Cranfield who has a belief that there is in store for him a mighty destiny which is to be confirmed by the appearance of three mysterious signs: first, he will discover his true love through her wearing "on her bosom a jewel in the shape of a heart"; second, a mighty treasure will be revealed to him by the sign of a hand pointing downward, "and beneath it the Latin word EFFODE—Dig"; finally, he will attain influence over his fellow man through some kind of extraordinary duty, the summons to which will be brought to him by "three venerable men."[15] After searching the whole world over for this destiny Ralph Cranfield at last returns to his native village to find the three prophecies fulfilled: his true love turns out to be his boyhood sweetheart, Faith Egerton; to discover the treasure, he is told to dig in the earth by his mother's dwelling, that is, to make a garden; and the three venerable men are the three village selectmen who offer Ralph the high destiny of village schoolmaster. Hawthorne concludes the tale with a longish moral in which he explicitly points out just exactly what he means by the various symbols.

To find the mysterious treasure, he was to till the earth around his mother's dwelling, and reap its products! Instead of warlike command, or regal or religious sway, he was to rule over the village children! And now the visionary Maid had faded from his fancy, and in her place he saw the playmate of his childhood! Would all who cherish such wild wishes but look around them, they would oftenest find their sphere of duty, of prosperity, and happiness, within those precincts and in that station where Providence itself has cast their lot. Happy they who read the riddle without a weary world search, or a lifetime spent in vain![16]

At this point the analogue to *Rasselas* becomes very striking. For like Ralph Cranfield Rasselas and his companions discover, after traveling the world over, that the best thing they can do is to return to the Happy Valley of Abyssinia. Now it is true that the tone of the two stories is different; Rasselas returns to Abyssinia with the explicit understanding that it is not the best of all imaginable, though it may well be the best of all possible, choices. The best of imaginable choices, he thinks, would be to be a ruler of a small kingdom. Similarly, the other characters in the story have unrealizable ideals which they would prefer to their actual lots. Pekuah would like to be the prioress of a nunnery; the princess would be happy with all knowledge for her province in the society of a college of learned women; and Imlac wishes that it were possible for him merely to drift along the stream of life. All these characters, however, discover their various ideals to be incapable of realization and return, at the end of the tale, to Abyssinia. Ralph Cranfield, on the other hand, returns to his village with a somewhat more optimistic viewpoint. The story does not carry the idea that Ralph has made a compromise with necessity; his idea of his high and noble destiny is gently ridiculed and the fact that he fulfills it as he does casts ridicule on his earlier ideal, not on its actual fulfillment.

Nevertheless, the stories are more different in tone than in actual meaning. Dr. Johnson, in *Rasselas*, also suggests that the ideals of Rasselas and his companions were unreal and incapable of fulfilment. The world is Abyssinia, as Rasselas finds out to his sorrow. Still, *Rasselas* is not a tragedy and Dr. Johnson never suggests that fate has in some way prepared an especially bitter blow for the Prince of Abyssinia. Both tales, in short, make a useful moral point, and the moral is generally the same: Unreal ideals are impossible of fulfillment on this earth and the wise man will discover that a realistic compromise is the only possible choice.

What I would like to suggest on the basis of this brief discussion is that Hawthorne uses the term "allegory" not as a statement of artistic means, in some sense roughly equatable with "symbolism," but rather as a statement of artistic ends, in some moralistic sense. An allegory for Hawthorne is a *moral tale,* and an equivalent for the term would be closer to "didactic" than to "symbolic." It is notable, whether or not the parallel with Dr. Johnson's *Rasselas* is convincing, that there are, in "The Threefold Destiny," no allegorical types at all, if allegory is interpreted as a kind of symbolism, although the story is explicitly called an allegory. The three signs of Ralph's destiny—the heart-shaped jewel, the hand pointing downward, and the three wise men— are not allegorical at all in this sense. Indeed, they are not even symbols in any meaningful way. They are perfectly definite statements of external circumstances which refer only to themselves and have only one function in the story, namely as clues to the outcome of the plot.

This is particularly notable in this tale since the three symbols could be very nicely allegorized without doing the story too much harm. The heart-shaped jewel—and Hawthorne is very fond of heart symbolism, which he uses on occasion in a very complex manner[17]—is a ready-made symbol for the sterling qualities of Faith Egerton, whose name also could be allegorically emphasized, as was the name of Young Goodman Brown's wife. The symbol of the downward-pointing hand with its Latin inscription could be usefully embellished by means of a pointed reference to its probable source, the concluding apothegm of the first part of *Candide,* that we should all cultivate our own gardens. Finally, the three venerable men could very easily be identified with the traditional symbol of the Magi, the three Fates, or the three wise men of Gotham. Nevertheless, valid as these symbols would be if Hawthorne had chosen to emphasize them, the point is that he did not choose to emphasize them, and certainly not in any allegorical fashion. If the story is an allegory in any sense at all it must be so in some way that has nothing to do with the symbolism. I have suggested, by comparing it to *Rasselas*, that the allegory in the tale is equivalent in Hawthorne's mind to the moral content of the story.

The peculiarly un-allegorical quality of those stories which might be considered to have symbolic allegorical content may best be seen by examining some of them. The case against Hawthorne's "allegory" can probably best be stated in terms of one inconsequential story, "The Antique Ring." This slight endeavor, of which Hawthorne thought so little that he did not include it in any collection of tales printed during his lifetime,[18] deals with a ring which one Mr. Edward Caryl gives to his betrothed, Clara Pemberton. Clara asks Caryl to tell her a tale about the ring, a tale which need not "be too scrupulous about facts."[19] Caryl's scruples, needless to say, are easily overcome, and he invents a long apocryphal tale about the ring's original owner which he tells to Clara and her friends.

In his reconstruction of the ring's history it develops that Queen Elizabeth had given the ring to the Earl of Essex as a mark of her favor, telling him that, if ever he fell into her disgrace, the ring might plead for him through an appeal to her mercy rather than to her sense of justice. Prior to this the ring had legendarily once belonged to Merlin the magician, who had imprisoned a fiend within its diamond. This fiend was compelled to work only good until some possessor of the ring should commit an evil deed, after which time the fiend would be free to work all the mischief he could until the ring again was purified by a holy or good action. The fiend, it is important to remark, had soon been released, for Merlin's lady-love, to whom he had given the ring, had rewarded his love by murdering him. At any rate, Essex, after being imprisoned in the Tower, gave the ring to the Countess of Shrewsbury, who promised to take it to the Queen. She betrayed his trust, however, and did not present the ring to Elizabeth, leaving him to go to his death without the ring's ever having spoken for him. Eventually, Caryl concludes, the ring was purified by being placed in the collection-box of an American church, shortly after which he had bought it for Clara.

The auditors of this rather jejune legend are extremely well pleased with it and ask Caryl for the meaning of the tale. He tells them, in no uncertain terms, that "we may suppose the Gem to be the human heart, and the Evil Spirit to be Falsehood, which, in one guise or another, is the fiend that causes all the sorrow and trouble in the world."[20] This is a plain enough allegorical statement of a one-for-one equation of a moral idea with an external symbol, but it is noteworthy that the only thing which Caryl explains in these allegorical terms is the ring itself. What about Essex, or the Countess of Shrewsbury, or the Queen? What have they to do with the tale; are they in some way allegorical types? The answer, I think, must be that they are not. Yet the story does have a definite *moral* content, being, if anything, a kind of expanded *exemplum* of a moral conceit. In addition, as we shall see by examining more of these tales, the "allegorical" symbol (in this case the ring) is not a device for giving the meaning of the tale so much as for introducing another kind of symbolic reality which goes counter to the expectations of the reader, and is both complementary and contradictory to the world of the story.

In "The Antique Ring" two completely different conceptions are combined, although it must be admitted with no great success. These are shown in this tale through the metaphor of the ring replete with attendant fiend and gloomy, irrational prophecy and, on the other side, the metaphor of Essex's conspiracy, the world of him and Elizabeth and the Countess of Shrewsbury, of human crime and treachery. Each of these metaphors forms a very good analogy to the other; both deal with human wrong under the aspect of treachery, but, and this is important, *in totally different ways*. In the tale the reality of "treachery" is a fact and Hawthorne discusses it under two headings: the treachery of Essex's conspiracy, which comprises his falseness to the Queen and the Countess of Shrewsbury's betrayal of him; and the mythical crime of Merlin's fiend who has been released by the treachery of Merlin's mistress.

All these metaphorical statements of treason and falsehood are, however, perceptible to the auditors only through the symbol of the ring itself, a symbol of the human heart with the evil spirit of falsehood imprisoned within it. The story, in other words, is neither *about* Essex nor *about* Merlin but about the ring, an emblem of the human heart. And the truth about the human heart which the two legends embody is that it has, inherent within it, falsehood. Yet this truth can be known only through the way the falsehood is made manifest, that is, in the story, through the legends of Essex and of Merlin. Truth, again, is only perceptible through its effects, for the ring in itself without Caryl's legends is meaningless.

Finally, these legends are different in kind. The legend of Essex's conspiracy is true to the laws of the Novel, to the world of everyday, of historical fact; the legend of Merlin and his murder and the release of the fiend is true to the laws of the Romance, the laws of the human heart, but unbound to the everyday world as we know it. Both of these legends, however, are equally true in their depiction of one aspect of the emblematic meaning of the ring, and Hawthorne again affirms in this tale the validity of two completely different modes of perception into a common reality.

This use of two diverse kinds of symbolism to give two distinct and quite different views of Reality may be more clearly seen in a better tale, "Egotism; or, the Bosom Serpent." This story, it will be recalled, was originally intended as one of a projected series of short stories to be called the "Allegories of the Heart." In its symbolic method it is remarkably similar to "The Antique Ring." Hawthorne assures us that the physical fact of a man swallowing a snake, "to which it is here attempted to give a *moral* signification, has been known to occur in more than one instance [italics mine]," as if to tie his allegory more closely to the facts of everyday experience. This solemn statement may or may not be true, though probably Hawthorne had some legendary idea in mind, since, as is well known, he was often stimulated by historical material of a definitely anecdotal cast.[21]

Whatever the factual basis to "Egotism" may have been, how-

ever, we can be fairly sure that Hawthorne changed it. Randall
Stewart has suggested that the idea of the snake comes from
The Faerie Queene, I, iv, 31, lines 3-5, a description of Envy.

> And in his bosome secretly there lay
> An hateful snake, the which his tale uptyes
> In many folds, and mortall sting implyes.[22]

Whether we equate the snake with "Envy" or with "Egotism"
actually matters little, since Hawthorne apparently makes a threefold equation: the snake equals Envy equals Egotism. Roderick
Elliston's friend Herkimer tells him after the snake has left his
bosom that it was symbolic of "a tremendous Egotism, manifest-
ing itself in your case in the form of jealousy."

As in the case of "The Antique Ring," then, we have at least
one clearly allegorical element in the tale, though, significantly,
its actual existence is problematical. The real presence of the
snake in Elliston's bosom, like the question of the reality of
Donatello's pointed ears, remains mysterious. Herkimer tells
Elliston, however, that "whether the serpent was a physical
reptile, or whether the morbidness of your nature suggested that
symbol to your fancy, the moral of the story is not the less true
and strong."[23]

The at least symbolic presence of this allegorical snake may,
nevertheless, cause the reader to overlook the fact that the story,
if an allegory, is a very curious one. The tale seems to be about
Roderick Elliston's deliverance from the sin of Egotism which is
symbolized by the snake he carries in his bosom. Elliston is
eventually cured of the disease, and rid of the snake, by being
brought to a condition where he is enabled to think of someone
other than himself, his wife Rosina. He humbles himself (and of
course Humility is death to Egotism, or Pride) by asking his wife's
forgiveness.

Though this story is a very moral tale, and though it deals
with a sin, Pride, which might be considered in theological terms,
the story does not deal with the sin in terms of simple allegory.
The snake may be allegorical; but if so, what is Roderick Elliston? All he can be is a type of either a man possessed by egotism,

or, more abstractly considered, of a man possessed by sin. Given this state of affairs, that a man is symbolically possessed by sin (and this, as I have attempted to show in Chapter II, is what we have to give the story more or less on faith), the plot of the tale works itself out on acceptable logical grounds. A man, Roderick Elliston, tortured by a secret egotism and separated by it from all mankind, is cured of it through the good offices of his wife and a friend, who, by presenting him with a consciousness of the enormity of his sin, enable him to conquer it through a recognition of his guilt and through his humble asking of pardon for it. After the cure is completed, the friend tells Elliston that whether or not the only allegorical symbol in the story has any real existence is *beside the point* of the tale.

In conclusion, if this story is an "Allegory of the Heart," it can only be so in some moralistic sense, in some way that it tells a truth about the heart in fictional terms. The method of telling the truth is not allegorical in the sense that heart-like qualities are equated with the characters in the tale. The closest one can come to an allegorical definition of the story is by putting the speculative question "Given a man possessed by Egotism, in this case symbolized by a snake in his bosom, how can he be cured?" In this tale the two perceptions into the nature of Reality are more successfully combined than they were in "The Antique Ring." The metaphorical snake in the bosom and the everyday world of Roderick Elliston are seen to be functions of one another. The irrational and the rational worlds are combined and seem to be cognate effects of an underlying truth. What the snake means in the world of the tale is true even though the snake himself, like the Devil in some religions, has only a metaphorical existence.

The peculiar quality of Hawthorne's irrational symbolism may be emphasized again by an examination of another of his "allegories," "Lady Eleanore's Mantle." In this story, Lady Eleanore, like Roderick Elliston in "Egotism," is a type of the proud human being. As a symbol of her overweening pride she wears an embroidered mantle which, it is rumored, has an almost magic power to give beauty to its wearer. At the end of the tale the mantle turns out to have been infected with smallpox and to have caused a disastrous epidemic which carried off not only the Lady Eleanore herself but a large portion of the population of Massachusetts as well. While on her deathbed Lady Eleanore comes to a realization of what the mantle symbolizes, and gives the moral of the tale in unambiguous terms: "The curse of Heaven hath stricken me, because I would not call man my brother, nor woman sister. I wrapped myself in PRIDE as in a MANTLE, and scorned the sympathies of nature; and therefore has nature made this wretched body the medium of a dreadful sympathy."[24]

Here again we have the equation: Pride equals, in this story at least, the Mantle, just as in "Egotism" Pride equaled the Serpent. But except for this one definite statement the allegorical frame of reference is meaningless, and any attempts to explain it make it all the more confusing. The name of Lady Eleanore's demented lover, Jervayse Helwyse, may be a pun on "Hell-wise," but if so, then what? He steals the sacramental cup and offers it to Lady Eleanore in a mysterious gesture of fellowship. Now does this all mean that the wisdom of Hell can conquer Pride by the sacrament of communion? Whatever it means it is certainly not that. Jervayse Helwyse is no more an allegorical type than is Lady Eleanore. Both are in some sense symbolic of Pride and its working on the human character; Lady Eleanore has isolated herself from common humanity until disease strikes her, reminding her of her "dreadful sympathy" with the rest of mankind. Jervayse, who is a sort of symbol of the Lady Eleanore's predicament, is himself isolated. Like her he is separated from the common bond of mankind, and his madness is not in kind much different from her Pride.

Both Lady Eleanore and Jervayse misunderstand reality. His coming to taunt her on her deathbed is a repayment in kind of her previous stepping on his prostrate body upon her arrival in Boston. Both actions show a singular lack of charity, and both characters through these actions act out the moral of the tale, which might be stated as "Pride goeth before a Fall." Still, once we give Hawthorne the initial oddity of the symbol in which he clothes his moral meaning the story works itself out in a perfectly logical way. Proud beauties are not confined to ıe pages of allegorical fiction; and a smallpox epidemic in the seventeeth century was only too common a human tragedy.

Andrew Schiller, in his brief analysis of "Wakefield," has compared Hawthorne to Kafka, and the comparison is a good one.[25] The artistic worlds of the two men and their respective use of symbols are remarkably close. In each case the author introduces an apparently allegorical symbol which does not function in an allegorical manner but is used only to emphasize some oddity—implied or expressed—of the characters in the story. The story, given this inital oddity, works itself out in a perfectly logical manner, indeed, in Kafka's case at least, often too logically.

The main difference between the two authors is that Kafka's symbols have lost any directly paraphrasable content, while Hawthorne's have not. We know, because Hawthorne tells us, what the snake and the mantle mean, at least intellectually. In contrast, we never discover just what is meant by the cockroach into which Gregor Samsa turns, though the effect of this transformation on his family becomes very clear in the course of the story.

Part of the terror of Kafka's story "Metamorphosis" is inherent in the fact that a family must deal with something which is apparently impossible, the transformation of the favorite son into a gigantic bug. And this terror is shown in a very calm way by Kafka's describing the daily life of this cockroach, how he is fed, how his room is cleaned, how he gets light and air, how all his other wants are supplied, how the family learns to adjust for him, and, most horrible of all, how the family tries to keep up appearances. Kafka does not attempt in this tale to suggest that there is any real danger of one of us turning into a bug. What he does, rather, is examine the impact of an unpleasant reality upon human beings who, it is painfully clear, cannot stand too much of it. The very ludicrousness of Kafka's symbol adds meaning to the tale in making its subject a kind of abstract and indefinable human trouble rather than murder or divorce or incest or whatever other specific ills humanity is heir to. In that we are all subject to the ills of mankind, Kafka suggests, we are all transformed Gregor Samsas, all loathsome insects beneath the skin.

The same conception, usually critically summarized as "secret sin," is basic to Hawthorne's vision, and it is here that his "allegory" is closest to Kafka's apparently irrational symbol. In all the "allegorical" tales of "secret sin," Hawthorne deals with symbols which border on the ludicrous. Lady Eleanore's mantle is about the most sane and commonsensical. More typical are the Reverend Mr. Hooper's black veil, Arthur Dimmesdale's burning heart, Roderick Elliston's snake, Miriam's spectre of the catacombs, Walter Ludlow's prophetic picture, and, most bizarre of all, the shroud in which Mr. Ellenwood marries Mrs. Dabney in "The Wedding Knell."

Finally, each author uses his symbols as a vehicle to convey unpleasant meanings in a commonsensical world. Summaries of some typical plots of both are amazingly alike in kind, and show each one's conscious attempt at an artistic effect by combining the ludicrous with the commonplace. The son of a respectable middle-class family turns into a cockroach and eventually dies; a man carries a snake in his bosom from which he is ultimately delivered; at a circus the crowd is entertained jointly by a panther and by a man who starves himself in public; a minister one day, for an apparent whim, appears in public wearing a black veil which he never again removes.

These tales could easily be by one author rather than two,[26] and, as I have attempted to show, are essentially the same in their symbolic reference. An apparently irrational and certainly improbable symbol is set against a plausible and everyday background for the purpose of exploiting the contrast between the commonplace and the apparently inexplicable, eventually showing that one is a function of the other. Just as we all carry snakes in our bosoms, so we are all Gregor Samsas. A world of commonplace good is contrasted with a world of bizarre, yet at least metaphorically explicable evil; and the two are shown to be inextricably related.

Another group of "allegories" in which Hawthorne occasionally deals are the satirical ones which poke fun at the various reform movements of his own time. These allegories, I believe, are no more allegorical in any symbolic sense than are the allegories discussed above. Of these satirical allegories I will discuss two, "Earth's Holocaust," and "The Celestial Railroad."

The first of these is scarcely even apparently allegorical in a symbolic sense, though Hawthorne tells us that "the illumination of the bonfire might reveal some profundity of moral truth heretofore hidden in mist or darkness." This bonfire of "wornout trumpery" is supposed to take place somewhere in the broad prairies of the West, "but whether in the time past or time to come" Hawthorne does not tell us.[27]

The locating of the bonfire in nowhere and everywhen is a typical Hawthornean device of abstracting the world of the tale from the everyday world and yet giving it at the same time a close contact with the appearances of daily life. The same device is used in "A Select Party" which takes place in a Castle in the Air, located, like the bonfire in this tale, both nowhen and everywhere. This beginning of the tale could very well progress into an allegorical burning of all the "wornout trumpery" of mankind, and in a sense it does. But actually, the sense is only a very specialized one. Given the initial absurdity of the tale—that there *is* a bonfire somewhere which is actually about to burn up all the excrescences of humanity—the story moves on with perfect logic.

The important point is that in this symbolic bonfire in this allegorical prairie divorced from real time and space it is *not* allegorical excrescences that are burned. What are thrown into this bonfire are the everyday realities themselves, and not their allegorical significances. The reformers begin by burning up old newspapers and worn-out heraldic symbols. Titles of nobility, orders of knighthood, and all the paraphernalia of hereditary rank are thrown helter-skelter into the fire. The point here is, however, that the real titles are thrown in, not their allegorical significations or any allegorical meanings. The only symbolic—in the sense of unreal or allegorical—element in the story is the bonfire into which the other objects are thrown.

The unreality of this bonfire is shown later when it begins to burn things selectively, refusing, for example, the Bible which "only assumed a more dazzling whiteness as the finger marks of human imperfection were purified away," though "certain

marginal notes and commentaries . . . yielded to the intensity
of the fiery test," albeit "without detriment to the smallest
syllable that had flamed from the pen of inspiration."[28] Similarly,
Shelley's poetry burns with "a purer light than almost any other
productions of his day," while Byron's burns with "fitful and lurid
gleams and gushes of black vapor."[29] It should again be emphasized that what is being burned here is not the moral quality
of the Bible or of Byron or Shelley but the actual works themselves, or, more exactly, both together. In this symbolic flame
the real products are being consumed by an allegorical fire,
not, as it would at first appear, the other way around.

In its symbolic structure, then, the story is very close to
the other allegories previously discussed. One symbolic element
is introduced, in this case the bonfire, in order to give an
air of unreality to the only too rational plot of the story. Given
the initial absurdity—that this bonfire could and did take
place and that all things were really burned up—the story works
itself out on an unexceptionably logical and rational basis. The
only unreal element is the situation of the story to start with,
the fact that this bonfire is, in a world where things are seen
just as they are, impossible.

"The Celestial Railroad" is, apparently at least, more nearly
a conventional allegory than is "Earth's Holocaust." This tale is
a satirical reworking of Bunyan which mocks the easy salvation
of Transcendentalism and modern "liberal" religion. As a parody
it is somewhat dangerous to discuss, since its form must to a
large extent depend upon that of the work it imitates. Still, if
the story is a take-off of Bunyan, it is a peculiar one. If "The
Celestial Railroad" is a satire of the Transcendentalists, Hawthorne strains at the allegorical form even within the rather
narrow formal limits required by his parody of *The Pilgrim's
Progress.*

First of all, the piece has the initial absurdity of the contrast
in manners. Mr. Smooth-it-away and the other passengers on the
Celestial Railroad are the most up-to-date specimens of mid-
nineteenth-century enlightenment, and are placed in immediate
ironic contrast to the two pilgrims toiling along the old hard
way toward the Celestial City. This aspect of the story as a

sort of costume-piece with a built-in joke on itself is completely foreign to the world of Bunyan's *The Pilgrim's Progress,* where no anachronism in time is at all felt. This anachronistic element of the tale is emphasized by the railroad itself, plowing across Bunyan's allegorical landscape, and is made even more emphatic by the replacement of Pope and Pagan by Giant Transcendentalist, who is, Hawthorne assures us, "a German by birth" and whom no one can understand because of the strangeness of his language.[30] The use of Bunyan's book as a guide to the landscape also provides its share of anachronistic humor, particularly since the landscape is not generally recognizable from the point of view of the railroad line, and Mr. Smooth-it-away has to point out the various historical monuments.

What has really happened in *The Pilgrim's Progress* in Hawthorne's hands is that the whole tone of the book has been changed, and the apparently allegorical characters are not allegorical at all. Where Bunyan's book is a metaphorical statement of a Christian man's progress to salvation, Hawthorne's tale is a take-off on Bunyan's machinery. Hawthorne never suggests in the tale that he is writing a guidebook to heaven or an edifying treatise, except insofar as any satire is indirectly edifying; his satire is peculiarly destructive, and not at all constructive.

As a result, his satirical characters, Mr. Smooth-it-away, the Rev. Mr. Shallow-deep, as well as the Tweedle-dum and Tweedle-dee of the story, the Rev. Mr. This-to-day and the Rev. Mr. That-to-morrow, along with the miscellaneous crowd of Mr. Scaly-conscience, Mr. Take-it-easy, the gentlemen from the town of Shun-repentance, and all of Hawthorne's other pseudo-Bunyanesque inventions have no meaning outside themselves. They are not allegorical characters standing for abstract moral virtues like Bunyan's Mr. Valiant-for-Truth or Hopeful, but rather purely pasteboard figures with no existence other than their names.

When Bunyan introduces an allegorical character, Valiant-for-Truth, for example, he does not simply introduce him and then let him drop. Valiant-for-Truth is made to show by his actions how a man acts who is valiant in the cause of truth. Similarly,

Doubtful engages Christian in a long conversation in which he shows how a doubtful man behaves in matters relating to his salvation. Hawthorne's characters never do this, with the possible exception of Mr. Smooth-it-away; they are merely counters at whose names we can chuckle. Rather than being allegorical figures they are animated puns.

The Pilgrim's Progress is a self-contained work of literature in that its meaning is evident without a knowledge of any other book, though some acquaintance with the Bible, while not completely indispensable, is desirable. "The Celestial Railroad," on the other hand, depends completely for its effect on the reader's knowledge of Bunyan. It is necessary for the reader to know how Bunyan employs his allegorical types in order for him to get any meaning at all out of "The Celestial Railroad," although the machinery of Bunyan's tale is so well imitated that the reader is at first unconscious of this.

The effect of Hawthorne's story again depends upon one of his favorite devices, the mixing of two modes of perception, the deceptively real and the metaphorically apparent, in this tale through the anachronistic symbolism of the Celestial Railroad. The humor of the story, and most of its effect, come from the incongruous mixing of the world of Bunyan's book with the mechanical improvements of Mr. Smooth-it-away. In this way the fable bears a very close resemblance to "Egotism" or to "The Minister's Black Veil." In all these tales the symbolism is basically the same in its operation, though the individual symbols are different enough. The irony in the character of the narrator of "The Celestial Railroad" lies in the fact that he comprehends within himself both worlds, the world of *The Pilgrim's Progress* and the world of the Celestial Railroad. The latter world is apparently the "real" one, though Hawthorne suggests that perhaps appearances are deceiving. Similarly, Roderick Elliston's snake and the transformed Gregor Samsa are emblematic of real worlds which are divorced from the apparent truths of everyday experience.

A passing discussion of "The Hall of Fantasy" will indicate how Hawthorne combines his satirical allegory with the theme of the organization of experience, discussed earlier in Chapter I.

The Hall of Fantasy, which exists in the same general geographical region as the bonfire of "Earth's Holocaust" and the Castle in the Air in which the Man of Fancy holds "A Select Party," is solemnly identified with the everyday world of commerce. It has "some of the characteristics of a public exchange," and we are assured that it "occupies in the world of fancy the same position which the Bourse, the Rialto, and the Exchange do in the commercial world."

In this Hall, of course, Hawthorne discovers many of the same characters who appeared at the Select Party, and he makes the point that the Hall is a meeting-place for "all who have affairs in that mystic region, which lies above, below, or beyond the actual."[31] In addition to the poets, philosophers and authors, though, accompanied by a group of scientists whose projects would be a credit to the Grand Academy of Lagado, there are present a number of men of business with fantastic schemes of progress. Hawthorne observes:

> There was a character of detail and matter of fact in their talk which concealed the extravagance of its purport, insomuch that the wildest schemes had the aspect of everyday realities. Thus the listener was not startled at the idea of cities to be built, as if by magic, in the heart of pathless forests; and of streets to be laid out where now the sea was tossing; and of mighty rivers to be stayed in their courses in order to turn the machinery of a cotton mill. It was only by an effort, and scarcely then, that the mind convinced itself that such speculations were as much matter of fantasy as the old dream of Eldorado, or as Mammon's Cave, or any other vision of gold ever conjured up by the imagination of needy poet or romantic adventurer.[32]

These men, in short, are just the ones to plan a Celestial Railroad.

In its basic meaning, this story is another fine example of Hawthorne's preoccupation with the reordering of experience, this time comically on the basis of fantasy rather than hardheaded practicality. Hawthorne's gentle satire makes the point that the "practical" man is often just as "fantastic" in a pejorative

sense as his more fanciful brethren. The lunatic, the poet, and
the businessman are, Hawthorne suggests, of imagination all
compact.

Combined with this theme, however, is the symbolic irony of
"The Celestial Railroad" and of Hawthorne's other "allegorical"
tales, the irony that the practical man is unable to understand
that these two worlds exist. This "practical" man is one with the
bespectacled gentleman in "Main Street" and the overly scientific
critic of Donatello's ears. He is unable to understand that there
is some validity in each of the two worlds of, say, Roderick
Elliston—the world of the snake in his bosom and the world in
which he lives—or of Lady Eleanore's Mantle and of seventeenth-century Boston. By confusing the two worlds, these
"practical" men come to a misapprehension of both. After
observing them for a while, Hawthorne sums up their condition:

> "Upon my word," said I, "it is dangerous to listen to such
> dreamers as these. Their madness is contagious."
> "Yes," said my friend, "because they mistake the Hall
> of Fantasy for actual brick and mortar, and its purple
> atmosphere for unsophisticated sunshine. But the poet
> knows his whereabout, and therefore is less likely to make
> a fool of himself in real life."[33]

For the poet knows the difference between the two worlds and
runs no risk of confusing them; he does not deny the existence of
one because it is apparently absurd.

It seems to me, in short, that much of the discussion of Hawthorne's "allegory" has suffered from a critical tendency to
make a rough equation between this term and "symbolism," while
Hawthorne would tend rather to equate "allegorical" with
"moral" or "didactic." Perhaps Hawthorne makes this equation
because of his habitual tendency to view art as a presentation in
veiled form of some kind of extra-experiential reality. Any
such theory of art would make art moral insofar as the reality
which it depicts is moral. If "moral" is a loaded term let us sub-
stitute "metaphysical" as a safer one. What I mean by this is
that Hawthorne's artistic aim is to give his reader some insight
into the world of ultimate reality, which by its very nature is

conceivable only in moral or metaphysical terms. I do not mean by this that Hawthorne's tales all make pat summaries of plat-itudinous ethical commonplaces, or that their moral content is by any means to be generally equated with sweetness and light; "Young Goodman Brown," "Roger Malvin's Burial," and "My Kinsman, Major Molyneux" give ample evidence to the contrary.

It is perhaps not too farfetched to suggest as well that "al-legorical" art, if we use the term as meaning "an equation of fictional characters with abstract moral qualities" is by its very nature moral, at least in any of the models Hawthorne knew. The symbol of the snake in "Egotism" may come from Spenser, and *The Faerie Queene* is certainly a moral work of art. "The Celestial Railroad" is an obvious imitation of Bunyan, and *The Pilgrim's Progress* is also a moral work. Though an allegory, in the sense in which these two works are allegories, must necessar-ily be a morality, it does not follow that any moral work must necessarily achieve its effect through allegorical means. Here is where the parallel to Dr. Johnson's *Rasselas* is instructive, whether or not the particular comparison of *Rasselas* to "The Threefold Destiny" is convincing. For both *Rasselas* and "The Threefold Destiny" are moral stories which eschew allegorical machinery, though they both tend toward an ethical meaning.

As for Hawthorne's "allegorical" symbols themselves, it would seem that they are, like Kafka's similar ones, used consciously for a ludicrous effect. By the intrusion of the incongruous into the world of everyday, Hawthorne attempts to suggest both the irrational and evil forces in man's nature and to show the contrast between the apparent and the real—artistic ends which at other times he achieves through the medium of the parable (as for example in "Young Goodman Brown," "My Kinsman, Major Molyneux," and "Roger Malvin's Burial") or of the incon-gruous tale dealing with the ordering of experience, such as "A Select Party," or "The Procession of Life," to mention only a few.

Hawthorne's symbols are "allegorical" in that they stand for a method of looking at experience which is not realistic. They are not allegorical in any sense of being primarily symbolic equations. And however allegorical they may be in the meanings which Hawthorne assigns them, their function in the tale is very peculiar. Functionally, these symbols are used to give a mode of perception which is, realistically at least, absurd, although paradoxically true. By combining these strange symbols in his tales with the world of everyday, Hawthorne is able to suggest two quite different yet equally valid ways of looking at a Reality which we are inclined to see only rationally because we are incapable of interpreting it in any other manner. Indeed, Hawthorne's insistence on the factual basis for many of his most wildly improbable stories represents a still more pointed assurance that the two apparently disparate worlds of everyday reality and fantastic symbol actually can and do interact upon occasion. Man's accidents are God's purposes.

Plot as a Vehicle
of Symbolic Meaning

WHEN George Parsons Lathrop sat down to write the Introductory Note to his edition of *The Ancestral Footstep* for inclusion in the Riverside Edition of Hawthorne's works, he was faced with something of a dilemma. *The Ancestral Footstep* was one of several obviously incomplete drafts of a romance which Hawthorne had left unfinished at his death. Lathrop was perplexed with problems of editorial policies, of notes, and most of all of arriving at some sort of workable idea of Hawthorne's methods of literary composition. He assumed, as did every critic until Edward Davidson published his edition of the posthumous works,[1] that *The Ancestral Footstep* was some kind of early draft of an English romance which was nearly finished in *Dr. Grimshawe's Secret.*

Without full knowledge of Hawthorne's various rough drafts and extensive revisions, Lathrop could ignore the problem of what the novel was about, but the question of literary method was not so easily disposed of. Lathrop assumed that Hawthorne wrote easily and directly—that he sat down, normally, to write a romance beginning at the first page and wrote straight through until the last. On the other hand, he was faced with direct evidence to the contrary in having what he considered to be the preliminary study for *Dr. Grimshawe's Secret* before him. His assumption was, therefore, that Hawthorne's method of work in composing *Dr. Grimshawe's Secret* had been somewhat exceptional. He decided finally:

It would not be safe to conclude, from the large amount
of preliminary writing done with a view to that romance,
that Hawthorne always adopted this laborious mode of
making several drafts of a book. On the contrary, it is
understood that his habit was to mature a design so
thoroughly in his mind before attempting to give it actual
existence on paper that but little rewriting was needed.
The circumstance that he was obliged to write so much
that did not satisfy him in this case may account partly
for his relinquishing the theme, as one which for him had
lost its seductiveness through too much recasting.[2]

This assumption has gone more or less unchallenged to the
present day, despite a good bit of evidence to the contrary. If
the design of the book were matured thoroughly in Hawthorne's
mind before it was written down on paper, certainly the plot at
least must have been definitely worked out. Yet Lathrop himself mentions at least once when this was not the case. "I believe
it has not before been recorded," he tells us, "that, when 'The
Scarlet Letter' had been written nearly through, the author
read the story aloud, as far as it was then completed, to Mrs.
Hawthorne; and, on her asking him what the ending was to be,
he replied: 'I don't know.'" A similar story, or just possibly the
same story told of a different tale is recounted by Julian Hawthorne of the composition of "Rappaccini's Daughter." According
to him, Hawthorne was reading the unfinished manuscript of
"Rappaccini's Daughter" to his wife in the Old Manse. To her
query "How is it to end?" he replied "I have no idea."[3]

Lathrop himself felt that the composition of *The Scarlet Letter*
was exceptional enough to warrant some explanation, which he
proceeded to offer. According to Lathrop, Hawthorne once
remarked to his sister-in-law, "'The difficulty is not *how* to say
things, but *what* to say'; implying that, whenever he began to
write, his subject was already so well developed as to make the
question mainly one of selection. But it is easy to understand how,
when he came to the final solution of a difficult problem, he might
then, being carried away by the conflicting interests of the different characters, hesitate as to the conclusion."[4] By minimizing the
area which Hawthorne still had left open to himself for free

discussion in his mind at the time of beginning a romance, Lathrop resolved the problem to at least his own satisfaction. Nonetheless, one is inclined to wonder if an alternative solution is not equally probable, the idea that because plot was unimportant to Hawthorne it could be left to take care of itself after other more central considerations.

It is certainly tempting to assume that Hawthorne normally composed in a straightforward, beginning-to-end fashion, especially since it gives at once a handy teleological view of Hawthorne's literary career and an apparently valid explanation of why the posthumous novels are unfinished, an explanation which assumes that Hawthorne, after the composition of *The Scarlet Letter*, gradually lost control of his plots. This position has been advanced by a number of critics, notably by Leland Schubert, who decides that Hawthorne's ability seems to have deteriorated as he grew older. Schubert concludes that, considered strictly on the basis of formal criteria, "the novels can be ranked *The Scarlet Letter*, *The House of the Seven Gables*, *The Blithedale Romance*, and lastly *The Marble Faun*,— the order in which the books were published. In other words, Hawthorne's skill in handling form in art seems to have diminished."[5]

There is undoubtedly a good deal of truth in this idea, carried only to a certain point. Obviously, the most glaring evidence of the lack of artistic control in the posthumous novels is that they are incomplete, fragmentary. At the risk of belaboring the obvious, the first requisite for a work of fiction—that it be in its own terms complete—is lacking. On the other hand, Schubert's assumption is inherently somewhat dangerous in that it is easy to assume from it that Hawthorne's ideal of form was necessarily the same as Schubert's, that is, that Hawthorne wrote with an ideal of form in mind which produced *The Scarlet Letter* as its masterwork.

This assumption lies behind many of the elaborate and often very perceptive analyses of form in *The Scarlet Letter* and *The House of the Seven Gables*. *The Scarlet Letter*, so the arguments run, is almost perfect structurally, and *Seven Gables* only slightly inferior. *Blithedale* represents a still further decline, and *The*

Marble Faun, with its "padding" of various kinds—art criticism, sight-seeing tours of Rome—and its generally hazy atmosphere, marks one further step down the inevitable road to the incomplete and futile posthumous romances.

Leland Schubert has nothing but praise for the structural excellence of *The Scarlet Letter*. He sees the "pattern of the story" as "clear and beautiful. It is built around the scaffold. At the beginning, in the middle, and at the end of the story the scaffold is the dominating point. Just as it literally rises above the market-place, so does it structurally rise out of the novel's plan and attribute pattern to it. In chapter two . . . Hester is taken up on the scaffold. In chapter twelve . . . Dimmesdale mounts the scaffold. In chapter twenty-three . . . Dimmesdale takes Hester and Pearl up there with him. These three incidents are, in every sense, the high points of the novel."[6] F. O. Matthiessen has arrived at somewhat the same conclusion. He accounts for the superiority of *The Scarlet Letter* on the grounds that "here Hawthorne has developed his most coherent plot. Its symmetrical design is built around the three scenes on the scaffold of the pillory."[7]

John C. Gerber sees that the "form of *The Scarlet Letter* is actually a four-part division, in each of which parts one character is central: in part one (Chapters I-VIII) the Puritan community; in part two (Chapters IX-XII) Chillingworth; in part three (Chapters XIII-XX) Hester; and in part four (Chapters XXI-XXIV) Dimmesdale.[8] Malcolm Cowley has gone even farther, and descried "a tragic drama divided into five big acts or tableaus, each of which is separated from the others by one or more brief scenes" in *The Scarlet Letter*, deciding that "it is on the five acts or tableaus that Hawthorne concentrated his talent as a stage designer and his mastery of lighting effect, not to mention his insight into the guilty heart." According to him, these five acts take place (1) in the market-place at Boston, when Hester Prynne is exposed to the populace, (2) in Dimmesdale's chamber, when Chillingworth is probing him in order to discover the cause of his mysterious illness, (3) in the market-place again, this time on the scaffold at midnight, (4) in the forest, and (5) again in the market-place, the final climactic scene where the meaning of the letter is revealed.[9] This five-act structure is actually not so different from the three-act structure discussed previously as might at first appear, since three of the five acts, as Cowley sees them, are the pivotal scenes around the scaffold in the market-place.

Discussions of the plot of *The House of the Seven Gables* have been, generally speaking, neither so ingenious nor so numerous as those of *The Scarlet Letter*, though Leland Schubert has found a complex proto-Joycean numerology in the novel which he does not feel is totally convincing.

> The facts are that *The House of the Seven Gables* does fit a pattern, and the number seven seems to be more than casually significant. There are seven principal characters: Hepzibah, Clifford, Jaffrey, Phoebe, Holgrave, Uncle Venner, and Ned Higgins. (If we want to push matters a bit, we can count seven characters from the past who wield a strong influence over the present: the original Maule, the builder Maule, the carpenter Maule; Alice; Colonel Pyncheon, the store-keeper Pyncheon, and Gervayse Pyncheon.) The twenty-one chapters of the novel can be divided structurally into three parts of seven chapters each.[10]

This is perhaps not directly referrable to the conception of "plot" at all; yet if the chapters of the novel can be divided structurally in any way which has meaning other than merely dividing twenty-one by seven, there must be some plot reference of some kind. Schubert mentions that the division is into three parts of seven chapters each, with the accent upon the *seven*. If we, on the other hand, put the accent upon the *three*, we have a three-act structure for *Seven Gables* close to that which Schubert finds in *The Scarlet Letter*.

Darrel Abel, on the other hand, feels that the romance is a five-act dramatization of the story of Naboth's vineyard in a modern version, the parable of "the contrived murder of a worthy poor man by his rich and great neighbor who coveted his small property."[11] The drama revolves around the symbol of the House which, according to Abel, is representative of "Tradition." The first act of the drama establishes this symbolic frame of reference. The second act describes the building of the House "and the defining of human relationships involved in its building."[12] The third act concerns itself with the House after the Pyncheons have built it, with it "in apparent prosperity still, but actually in incipient decay."[13] Act four brings us to "the present" of the story, with the house in an advanced state of decline; and act five, the climactic one, shows the fall of the House, the collapse of the "tradition," and its replacement by a new one. The Pyncheons, symbolically, are replaced by the Maules, and the oft-discussed "happy ending" is actually a new beginning.

The Blithedale Romance, probably because of a widespread critical opinion that it is the weakest of Hawthorne's long works, has received comparatively little discussion in terms of plot. Most analyses of the romance have concerned themselves with its autobiographical or historic significance or with its use of some of Hawthorne's favorite themes. And, ever since Trollope's well-meant censure that "the great fault" of *The Marble Faun* "lies in the absence of arranged plot,"[14] this romance has remained the despair of critics. Darrel Abel, its most perceptive modern critic, has assumed that its unity is a unity in terms of thematic meaning rather than of plot, and most other scholars have tended to agree with him.

To summarize the argument, then, what seems to me to have happened in interpretations of Hawthorne's plots is that the cart has been placed before the horse. It may be true that *The Scarlet Letter* has the finest plot of any of Hawthorne's novels. It is certainly true that an understanding of the beauty of the plot contributes to an understanding of the beauty of the work. But it does not follow from this that Hawthorne himself was particularly interested in the plots of his novels. To decide that *The Marble Faun* is inferior to *The Scarlet Letter* because its plot is more diffuse seems to me to mistake an accidental quality for an essential one, just as to say that the failure of the posthumous romances is due to Hawthorne's inability to handle their plots, without any attempt to assess any other factors.

Actually, in addition to the perhaps apocryphal anecdotes

of his not knowing how a story was going to end when he sat
down to write it, there is considerable indirect evidence that
Hawthorne did not care about his plots, but considered them
least in importance of all the elements of his artistry. E. H.
Davidson has shown that, in the fragments of the various posthumous romances, plot and character were shuffled around
ceaselessly, and that Hawthorne's only two really constant
preoccupations were with the idea of the "American who came
back to his forefathers' home in England and there busied himself with proving that he was the rightful heir to an old manor
house and the legend of the bloody footprint which Hawthorne
had heard from Mrs. Ainsworth of Smithell's Hall."[15]

To these themes we may add two more, the idea of the
Elixir of Life and of the Deathless Man. These two latter themes,
at least, had a long history in Hawthorne's mind. Early in his
artistic career he had written "Dr. Heidegger's Experiment,"
his first, and destined to be his only, published probing of the
problem of the elixir of life, and his interest in the subject
first appears in his Notebooks at about this time.[16] Without too
much exaggeration I think that one might say that the first
studies for the romance of immortality are not those which
Professor Davidson gives, but rather the entries in the Notebooks and the published tale, "Dr. Heidegger's Experiment."

What I am trying to suggest is that Hawthorne normally rewrote his stories, and that the preliminary sketches which Professor Davidson has discovered are probably no different in
kind from what Hawthorne presumably did in his earlier novels.
Arlin Turner has made the most thorough study of which I am
aware of Hawthorne's use of his source materials.[17] He has,
on the basis of his study of the Notebooks, decided that Hawthorne does not really write in terms of plot at all, but rather
in terms of accretion of detail around images which strike him,
and which go to illustrate some dominant idea. "Few, if any of
his works, including the novels and longer tales, can be said to
contain true plots; nor do many of them depend for interest
on a chronological sequence of events and the suspense resulting
from such an arrangement. Instead, most of them are composed
of several situations—several scenes, it may be, or various

episodes from the lives of the characters—all of which illustrate the dominant idea."[18]

Turner sees no apparent difference in Hawthorne's handling of his materials between the tales and the romances except that the tales are shorter. But, significantly, the tales are not shorter in number of incidents so much as in the accretion of detail around each incident. Thus Turner sees "Wakefield" as "an example in miniature of Hawthorne's method of planning his romances . . . 'Wakefield' is composed of a sequence of highlights from the twenty years embraced by the narrative: Wakefield's leaving home and establishing himself in an apartment in the same block; his decision not to return home on the following morning; his meeting his wife on the street ten years later; and his returning home, after an absence of twenty years." Like "Wakefield," Turner suggests, *The Scarlet Letter* is composed of a series of important scenes from the lives of Hester Prynne and Arthur Dimmesdale." He concludes:

> This comparison between the novel and "Wakefield" gains significance from the fact that *The Scarlet Letter* was first intended as one in a collection of tales. We can easily envisage the novel as a short narrative. Only the more important scenes would be touched on, and they would be much shorter than at present. Yet nothing of the framework or meaning of the romance would be sacrificed; the difference would be that fewer and briefer manifestations of the theme could be included.[19]

Turner's suggestion that Hawthorne originally composed *The Scarlet Letter* in a series of narrative blocks, with the implicit corollary that this was his normal method of working, is significant in that it suggests that the plot was of practically no importance in itself to Hawthorne. The important thing to him was the complex of meaning inherent in the narrative block rather than the way all the narrative blocks hung together to form a whole.

This is a better explanation of why Hawthorne was uncertain of the end of *The Scarlet Letter* than the one Lathrop gives. For it would seem that Hawthorne was not much interested in whether Hester and Dimmesdale lived happily ever after, or whether some other ending was chosen. And it is not by accident that the ending with which Hawthorne finally concluded the romance was the most indefinite one possible. It is a conclusion which solves none of the problems raised by the book except by rendering them unanswerable. We do not know at the end of the tale whether or not Hester's and Dimmesdale's sin had a consecration of its own, and we are not intended to know it. Hawthorne ends the tale in a merely temporal fashion, purposely avoiding any implication by means of the outcome of the plot as to what our attitude toward the three main characters should be. He finishes the romance as he had begun it, by insisting on the importance of the Scarlet Letter, and by steadfastly refusing to explain what this importance is.

The meaning of *The Scarlet Letter,* in other words, is not shown through the development of the plot of the romance, but rather through the consistently developed and ultimately mysterious multiple significance inherent in the Letter itself. The plot of the tale becomes a device by which the enigmatic Letter is shown in some of its many meanings. The development of the story is a development in terms of an unknowable symbol and not in terms of a rational plot.

The whole prior history of the concept of the Scarlet Letter emphasizes this fact: that the symbol is basic to the plot and not the plot to the symbol. The first mention of the idea of the Scarlet Letter as the central theme for a tale appears in the *American Notebooks* some time shortly after October 13, 1844, yet before March 12, 1845. Hawthorne jots down in the Notebooks the entry, "The life of a woman, who by the old colony law, was condemned always to wear the letter A, sewed on her garment, in token of her having committed adultery."[20] This is an elaboration of one incident in Hawthorne's early story, "Endicott and the Red Cross," written probably in the Winter of 1837. In this tale, one of the observers of Endicott's desecration of the flag was "a young woman . . . whose doom it was to wear the letter A on the breast of her gown, in the eyes of all the world and her own children. . . . Sporting with her infamy, the lost and desperate creature had embroidered the fatal token in scarlet cloth, with golden thread and the nicest art of needlework; so that the capital A might have been thought to mean Admirable, or anything rather than Adulteress."[21] Some time between the date of this story and the notebook entry, Hawthorne had decided that this apparently extraneous detail of the Scarlet Letter, used in "Endicott" only as a kind of ironic "local color" with which to contrast this woman, along with the other outcasts, with Endicott's impassioned pleas for liberty, could be made to bear sufficient symbolic weight to be the subject of a tale.

Hawthorne's similar revisions of source material in the Notebooks shows an analogous concern with a constant increase of the symbolic meaning of his images. C. A. Reilly has shown how Hawthorne reworked the journal entry of the dog chasing his tail for inclusion in "Ethan Brand."[22] He points out that in addition to using more dignified words in the story than appeared in the notebook entry, Hawthorne has "made the dog of the story seem more human and at the same time more absurd" than his original, and has made him roughly parallel to Ethan Brand, at least in the absurdity of their two quests—the dog for his tail, Ethan Brand for the Unpardonable Sin. Furthermore, the notebook entry has been greatly expanded in the tale, being, in its final form, about twice as long, and the entry has actually been changed a bit for "Ethan Brand," since the dog in the Notebooks had actually succeeded in catching his tail, whereas in "Ethan Brand" he remains frustrated. Certainly Hawthorne had some purpose in rewriting this passage as he did, and he, at least, must have thought that the revision added some significance, symbolic or otherwise, to the tale.

Indeed, Hawthorne was sometimes not pleased with the way in which he was handling his preliminary material in the Notebooks, so that even his arduous self-examination in the sketches for the posthumous works, which Davidson finds so significant, seems to be a normal procedure.[23] The sketch "The Old Apple Dealer," for example, is based almost entirely on one long notebook entry for January 23, 1842.[24] Some time between this date and January, 1843, when the essay was published, Hawthorne rewrote it, leaving his basic conception intact. Most interesting is that Hawthorne, in his Notebook description of the old man, was conscious that he had not captured the effect which he wished. He writes:

> After all this description, I have not expressed the aspect and character of the old man, in anything like a satisfactory manner. It requires a very delicate pencil to depict a portrait which has so much of negative in it—where every touch must be kept down, or else you destroy the subdued tone, which is most essential to the character.

And he goes on to describe how he will develop the character further if he ever writes the sketch up for publication.

> Now imagine this old man, so subdued, so hopeless, so without a stake in the world—and yet not positively miserable—this old man, wearing out dismal day after dismal day, over his little stock of apples and candy—imagine him sitting in the Station house, in the very midst of the bustle and movement of the world, when all our go-ahead stream of population rushes and roars along beside him. Travelers from afar, travelers going up to Boston business, young men on a pleasure-jaunt—all sorts of various people sweep by him; and there he remains, nervous, chill, patient.[25]

When Hawthorne came to write the sketch "The Old Apple Dealer" he followed his own suggestions given in this last quotation. The apple dealer himself is used as a foil to all the travelers and scurrying businessmen who hurry hither and yon by the train. He is a kind of metaphorical still point in a turning world, and both he and the various travelers cast an ironic light upon each other.

> The travellers swarm forth from the cars. All are full of the momentum which they have caught from their mode of conveyance. It seems as if the whole world, both morally and physically, were detached from its old standfasts and set in rapid motion. And, in the midst of this terrible activity, there sits the old man of gingerbread; so subdued, so hopeless, so without a stake in life, and yet not pos-

itively miserable,—there he sits, the forlorn old creature, one chill and sombre day after another, gathering scanty coppers for his cakes, apples and candy,—there sits the old apple dealer, in his threadbare suit of snuff color and gray and his grizzly stubble beard . . . I have him now. He and the steam fiend are each other's antipodes; the latter's the type of all that go ahead, and the old man the representative of that melancholy class who, by some sad witchcraft, are doomed never to share in the world's exulting progress. Thus the contrast between mankind and this desolate brother becomes picturesque, and even sublime.[26]

Nevertheless, Hawthorne is still uneasy about his inability to catch precisely the tone he wishes for in the description of the old man. He begins the sketch with a half-apologetic sentence, "The lover of the moral picturesque may sometimes find what he seeks in a character which is nevertheless of too negative a description to be seized upon and represented to the imaginative vision by word painting,"[27] and goes on to explain that the old apple dealer is such a man. Somewhat further on in the sketch Hawthorne confesses that he has not completely solved the artistic problem of presenting the old man's character, in a passage which still bears a very close resemblance to its original in the Notebooks.

> To confess the truth, it is not the easiest matter in the world to define and individualize a character like this which we are now handling. The portrait must be so generally negative that the most delicate pencil is likely to spoil it by introducing some too positive tint. Every touch must be kept down, or else you destroy the subdued tone which is absolutely essential to the whole effect.[28]

Another bit of evidence of this self-criticism may be found in the tale "The Christmas Banquet." This tale, along with "Egotism; or, the Bosom Serpent," was originally planned as part of the unrealized collection of short stories to be called "Allegories of the Heart." It depicts Roderick Elliston, after his regeneration from the snake in his bosom, in the role of artist.

He has written a tale of a Christmas banquet which he proceeds to read to his wife and to his friend Herkimer. Before starting, however, he gives a preamble to the tale by telling something about its protagonist, Gervayse Hastings, who is the only permanent guest at the annual banquet of the most miserable. He is, Roderick says, a man who lacks any human warmth; his heart is not so much hard as it is cold, and Roderick suggests that if such a man were, "what, probably, he never is,—conscious of the deficiency in his spiritual organization," he would have as a result "a sense of cold unreality wherewith he would go shivering through the world, longing to exchange his load of ice for any burden of real grief that fate could fling upon a human being."[29]

In the course of the tale, Gervayse Hastings personifies such a man, to the best of Roderick Elliston's artistic skill in portraying him. At the end of the story Roderick asks Rosina for her criticism of his effort, and she replies that his success is "by no means complete," since her idea of the character of Gervayse, she says, comes "rather by dint of my own thought than your expression."

This is exactly the criticism which Hawthorne makes of his own attempt at the portrayal of the apple dealer, and the characters of Gervayse Hastings and the old apple dealer are by no means so disparate as they might at first appear. The artistic problem in their presentation is in both cases the same, that of presenting a negative character in positive terms. Roderick answers his wife's criticism by saying that it is "unavoidable," since Gervayse's characteristics are "all negative." He concludes that "if Gervayse Hastings could have imbibed one human grief at the gloomy banquet, the task of describing him would have been infinitely easier."[30] Hawthorne, as a "lover of the moral picturesque," feels obliged to depict the character of the old apple dealer, and, by extension, of Gervayse Hastings, though he is nonetheless doubtful of his ability to do so in artistic terms.

Composition, then, was for Hawthorne not an easy art, and he probably did not just sit down and dash off a tale when he felt that he understood it perfectly. E. H. Davidson's discussion

of Hawthorne's methods of writing, based on the drafts and
preliminary sketches for the posthumous works, has led him to
conclude that Hawthorne began to compose with a moral idea in
his mind, this moral idea being what is generally first put down
in the Notebooks. After Hawthorne had once conceived of this
moral idea, he merged it with an image, "the two fused into
a symbol, and from that merging automatically came characters,
scene and plot."[31] Arlin Turner, on the basis of his study of the
Notebooks, but without benefits of the preliminary drafts for
the posthumous works, has arrived at similar conclusions
regarding Hawthorne's methods of composition.

> He began every piece with a basic idea, which came to
> him in connection with some physical manifestation. He
> then expanded the idea, narrowed it down, or altered it
> in other ways until he had a clearly defined plan. The
> development of this plan ordinarily consisted of choosing
> and placing in some sort of a procession a series of scenes
> or incidents to represent the theme. Each scene or episode
> he filled in by details of characterization, action, and setting
> drawn mainly from his own observation, the whole, how-
> ever, carefully surrounded by a vague, and romantic atmos-
> phere to isolate it from the world of reality.[32]

One may legitimately take exception, however, to Davidson's
further conclusion that "all circumstances and themes had to be
just right," and the implication in the following statement that
"when the process worked in those inner recesses of [Haw-
thorne's] imagination, the novel wrote itself."[33] This idea assumes
that Hawthorne either wrote easily or not at all, ignoring the
possibility that he might—as I suggest he did—normally write
with great pain and not at all facilely, revising constantly.

Davidson seems to assume that because no early drafts of the
four completed romances exist Hawthorne wrote them up quite
quickly and easily. It seems that on the purely negative evidence
that we have none of these drafts, Davidson has repeated George
Parsons Lathrop's conclusion that Hawthorne normally did not
write sketches and rough drafts for his works. I suggest rather
that Hawthorne *did* write preliminary drafts—how many we have

no idea—of his romances, and that the discovery of the rough drafts for the incomplete posthumous works serves not so much to prove that Hawthorne was at loose ends about the completion of either the "Romance of Immortality" or the "Romance of the Lost Heir" as to indicate, coupled with the evidence of the evolution of his ideas from first notebook entry to finished story or romance, that Hawthorne normally rewrote and revised his material at great length. Just because we have no preliminary drafts for any of the other romances is no certain proof that there were none.

I have attempted to show that at least two slight preliminary sketches of *The Scarlet Letter* did exist, the notebook entry and the tale "Endicott and the Red Cross." In addition, there is some evidence that there was at least one incomplete draft of *The Marble Faun*. Hawthorne wrote to William D. Ticknor, on March 4, 1859, that he had "written a Romance," but that "it still requires a good deal of revision, trimming off of exuberances, and filling up of vacant spaces; but I think it will be all right in a month or two after I arrive."[34] This indicates that Hawthorne's rough draft of *The Marble Faun* was actually similar to the incomplete romances. It would appear that it was written, as they were, in narrative blocks, with summaries of the "vacant space" to which Hawthorne would return later for further revision. And this despite the fact that *The Marble Faun*, from first conception to final form, was written in a much shorter time than any of Hawthorne's earlier romances, though it is twice as long.

The Marble Faun could not have had its inception before the end of January, 1858, when Hawthorne and his family arrived in Rome. Since the romance was finished in March of 1860, this gives at the outside a twenty-six-month period of composition, reckoned from initial inception to completion. On the other hand, the first record of *The Scarlet Letter* we have is the story "Endicott and the Red Cross," which was probably written in the winter of 1837 but may have been written as early as 1834. We know certainly that it was completed by June of 1837. *The Scarlet Letter* itself was published in April, 1850, though it had been finished by February 3rd of that year. In other words, the theme of the book had been floating in Hawthorne's mind for something over thirteen years, even taking the latest possible estimate for the date of composition of "Endicott and the Red Cross."

On *The House of the Seven Gables* such exact speculation is doubtful, though various elements in the tale go back to jottings in the Notebooks from as early as 1848 and 1849.[35] *Blithedale,* on the other hand, very obviously dates from Hawthorne's stay at Brook Farm from April to November, 1841. *Blithedale* was published in June, 1852, though probably finished in May of that year, showing that it had been lying fallow in Hawthorne's mind for a comfortable eleven years. The theme of the elixir of life, which Hawthorne was working into his posthumous romances, has a similar venerable history. Without bothering to trace all the various entries in the Notebooks, one need only remark that "Dr. Heidegger's Experiment" was written some time between December, 1834 and February, 1837.

Hawthorne's contemporaries were well aware of his tendency to rewrite and upon occasion to overwrite his materials, though they of course had no proof that he wrote many drafts to his various tales and romances. The more acute of these critics saw that Hawthorne's concern with detail represented a conscious effort to produce a certain artistic effect, and that his stories did not depend to any great extent upon plot interest. His sister-in-law, Elizabeth Peabody, writing a joint review of his works and his son Julian's, in 1875, says of him that he "seems to lack invention of story, and characterization of individualities. His incidents are for the most part every-day ones, and often disconnected. . . . Hence the personages of his romances are hardly individuals of palpable flesh and blood, but rather ideas and symbols of the universal facts of human nature."[36]

One might consider this statement as a quasi-official family view, especially in light of a similar statement by Julian Hawthorne that his father's stories "depend but in a subordinate degree upon what is called technically plot interest. The author's method was to take a natural, even a familiar incident, and to transmute it into immortal gold by simply elucidating its inner spiritual significance."[37] Julian's rhetoric has confused the statement perhaps unnecessarily. The "immortal gold" of Hawthorne's tales, though, seems to be fairly nearly synonomous with the "universal facts of human nature" which Elizabeth Peabody mentions. In other words, both state that Hawthorne has what a modern critic has called a "graphic" mind, that is, that "he thinks in pictures."[38] These pictures, which are the matter of his tales, are more important to him than the overall form. Actually, this is probably somewhat an overstatement of the case. The plot is not unimportant to Hawthorne, but it is important primarily as a vehicle for meaning, "as the outward, bodily sign of inward and moral drama."[39]

Perhaps most interesting of all in this connection is an early review of *The House of The Seven Gables* by Henry Chorley in the *Athenaeum* for May 24, 1851. This review is generally favorable. Chorley prefers this romance to *The Scarlet Letter*, and is generally complimentary to Hawthorne. He concludes his review, however, with a precautionary statement that Hawthorne's love of detail may cause a decline in his art. Chorley sees this love of detail as a blemish, though he understands why Hawthorne is so fond of it. As a device, he approves of it, warning Hawthorne only against letting it run away with him.

> Before . . . we leave this book, we have to note a fault in it, not chargeable upon 'The Scarlet Letter,'—and one which . . . we mention in friendly jealousy, lest it grow into a habit. . . . That affluence of fancy, that delight in playing with an idea and placing it in every chameleon light of the prism, and that love of reverie, which are so fascinating in a humourous essayist—become importunate if employed in scenes of emotion and junctures of breathless suspense. The speculations, for instance, upon him who sat in the deserted house on the day of the catastrophe fret the reader with their prosy and tantalizing ingenuity. They would have been in their place in the study of a single figure; but as interrupting the current which is sweeping the fortunes of many persons to the brink of the cataract— they are frivolous and vexatious. We beg our vigorous inventer and finely finished artist (Mr. Hawthorne is both) to mistrust himself whenever he comes to his second simile and his third suggestion. They weaken the reader's faith,—

they exhaust, not encourage, in that desire to consider "what might have happened" in such or such cases which it is so essentially the privilege of first-class stories to generate.[40]

Here, rather than in the failure of the artist to control his plot, is the crux of the whole matter. Even if we accept with most modern critics the highly doubtful assumption that there was something in Hawthorne's makeup which prevented him from finishing the posthumous romances—whether neuroses, anxiety, old age, monetary worries or illness make very little difference—to lay the cause of Hawthorne's failure on his inability to control the plot of these tales is to misinterpret what has really happened.

It is true that Hawthorne did not finish the plots of the posthumous romances, although in actual fact he suggested conclusions for each one. It is not so much that he was unable to finish the romances as that he didn't really *want* to until he had said everything possible to be said about every imaginable aspect of every single symbol. He apparently wanted, in these last romances, to get everything possible said, only to find that this was an unattainable object. As Professor Davidson has pointed out, Hawthorne rewrites the "Romance of Immorality" "to an incredible degree," and without covering any particularly new ground. One does wonder, along with Professor Davidson, "if Hawthorne will ever be able to move from one scene to another,"[41] but one wonders not from the standpoint of whether or not Hawthorne *can* move, but from the point of view of whether or not he *will*. Hawthorne is perfectly capable of moving on from one part of his story to another if he once thinks that he has said everything important about the first part. The hitch comes in his unwillingness to leave anything incomplete, anything at all unsaid.

One might compare Hawthorne's problem here with the problem Joyce later faced successfully in *Ulysses* and rather less so in *Finnegans Wake*. In *Ulysses*, first of all through the limiting of time to one day in the life of his two heroes, and through the contributory aids of classic mythological parallels, stylistic analogies, numerology, religious and sexual symbolism, artistic criticism and God knows what all else, Joyce has attempted to tell everything possible about Stephen Dedalus and Leopold Bloom. It is almost as if Hawthorne stumbled upon this principle unawares. Like Joyce, he began by writing "epiphanies" and ended by an ever-expanded and expanding epiphany which became all-inclusive.

I have already briefly indicated the history of the symbol of the Scarlet Letter, suggesting that its meanings constantly proliferated in Hawthorne's mind as he mulled over its enigmatic significance. The best example, however, of Hawthorne's constant concern with the elaboration of symbolic significance may be found in the development of the theme of the elixir of life, the never-completed romance of the "Deathless Man."

Hawthorne's first, and destined to be his only, published exploration of this theme was "Dr. Heidegger's Experiment." In this tale, the general philosophic idea underlying the various previous notebook entries, that the search for the elixir of life and its discovery would be disastrous, is practically unchanged. The Doctor himself is more or less overtly Hawthorne's mouthpiece, and the story revolves around the pathetic result of the discovery of the elixir of life. Dr. Heidegger has concocted this elixir and proposed to his four aged contemporaries that they drink it. He warns them that perhaps it would be well, before they drink, for them to "draw up a few general rules for . . . guidance, in passing a second time through the perils of youth," but the old people, chuckling tremulously, feel that this is unnecessary. When once rejuvenated by the water, they commit the same follies which they had committed in their first youth, proving that their lives have taught them nothing. The joys of youth, for these old people, are the only real joys which exist, and at the end of the tale they decide to set out for Florida in order to discover the whereabouts of the fountain of youth.

The Doctor himself has placed his attitude toward the fountain of youth and its rejuvenating powers in direct contrast to the attitudes of his four futile old acquaintances, by declining to drink its waters with the polite, yet significant statement that "having had much trouble in growing old, I am in no hurry to grow young again."[42] At the end of the tale, the Doctor has been taught by the antics of his friends that youthful joys are an illusion. The effect of the water of youth is not valuable to a truly wise man. Dr. Heidegger realizes that the joys of youth must by their very nature die, like their emblem, the rose given him by his long-dead sweetheart, which blooms and then fades. But because they cannot last forever is no real reason to lament their going; the Doctor loves the shrivelled rose as well as he had loved the budding flower. And he has no lament to give for the water of youth, which in the mad struggles of the four temporarily rejuvenated elders, has been spilled upon the floor.

> "Yes, friends, ye are old again," said Dr. Heidegger, "and lo! the Water of Youth is all lavished on the ground. Well—I bemoan it not; for if the fountain gushed at my very doorstep, I would not stoop to bathe my lips in it—no, though its delirium were for years instead of moments."[43]

Dr. Heidegger, through the symbol of his fiancée's decayed rose, has realized what the others cannot comprehend, that, in the biblical phrase, for all things there is a season. There is a time to make love and a time to die, and it were better for man not to attempt to change the seasons which have been ordained to all things. Earth's happiness is as brief as the flowering of a rose, and the wise man had better think on eternity.

Whether or not we approve of the moral which Hawthorne draws from this examination of the problem of eternal youth-fulness, we may well be appalled at the superficiality of his treatment of the theme. Somehow we know how the story is going to end even before we have really begun to read it, and it becomes painfully clear that these old people, at least, have no right to the possession of eternal youth. Similarly, Dr. Hei-degger's refusal to drink the water of the fountain of youth and his peroration at the end of the tale might just as well have sprung from disgust with the revolting spectacle of three elderly roués and a superannuated belle cavorting senselessly in his chambers as from any deep conviction of the vanity of eternal youth. The reader can scarcely help asking, "*Is* there no possible justification for wanting to live forever?" or, rather, he is prepared to admit that the four old people certainly are not worth the gift of eternal life or eternal youth, but that this story does not explore the problem sufficiently. Must everyone be like these four aged epicures? Are they the *only* representative types?[44]

Some such question seems to have motivated Hawthorne when he sat down to investigate the theme of the elixir of life further in the two posthumous romances which deal directly with the "Deathless Man." The first of these, *Septimius Felton*,[45] portrays a favorite Hawthornean villain, the selfish, scientific, cold-hearted man portrayed before in the characters of Ethan Brand and Rappaccini. Septimius Felton himself, however, is apparently not so much a villain as a deluded idealistic scientist, and perhaps his nearer prototype would be Aylmer in "The Birthmark." At any rate, he is a more satisfactory human universal than are the four old people of "Dr. Heidegger's Experiment."

The plot of *Septimius Felton* hinges on two great ironies. The first of these, which is discovered only at the end of the tale, and which Hawthorne apparently never worked out completely in his own mind, is that the whole affair is a cheat. Like the water of the fountain of youth, the elixir of life is not real but delusory. It is certain that Hawthorne intended to make the search for the elixir into an ironic wild-goose chase, though just how he was going to do it is uncertain, whether through killing Septimius, or Sibyl Dacy, or spilling the elixir *à la* Dr. Heidegger, or, possibly, through some other means.

The more important irony, however, is the irony of the life in death which Septimius must live in order to find this elixir. For the elixir cannot only be made, it must be lived. Septimius must order his existence on a practically monastic basis, and while searching with his whole spirit for the recipe which will grant him a future existence must be content to lose his present one. These ironies, of course, are brought together in the catastrophe at the end when Septimius finds not only that the elixir is a cheat, but that he has wasted his life in useless research. He is in a very real sense in the predicament of the nameless hero of an unrealized story which exists only in the Notebooks.

A young man finds a portion of the skeleton of a Mammoth; he begins by degrees to become interested in completing it; searches round the world for the means of doing so; spends youth and manhood in the pursuit; and in old age has nothing to show for his life but this skeleton.[46]

The notebook entry could stand for a plot summary of *Septimius Felton* if instead of searching for a mammoth the youth had begun his search for the elixir of life. In their futility, the search for the skeleton of a mammoth and the search for the elixir of life are about on a par.

The irony of sacrificing one's life for an unsure future good, which is the pervading metaphor of the book, is worth some further discussion. Septimius is expected to order his life according to certain precepts which appear on the surface to embrace an admirable kind of stoicism, but actually are nothing more than a subtle guise for a rather unenlightened self-interest presented in universal terms. The general tendency of these precepts also leads to estrangement from mankind, making the point that to live forever is the same as not really living at all. Among other precepts to which the wise man should order his life are the following, chosen deliberately as being the most ludicrous.

"Kiss no woman if her lips be red; look not upon her if she be very fair. Touch not her hand if thy finger-tips be found to thrill with hers ever so little. On the whole, shun woman, for she is apt to be a disturbing influence. If thou love her, all is over, and thy whole past and remaining labor and pains will be in vain.

"Do some decent degree of good and kindness in thy daily life, for the result is a slight pleasurable sense that will seem to warm and delectate thee with felicitous self-laudings; and all that brings thy thoughts to thyself tends to invigorate that central principle by the growth of which thou art to give thyself indefinite life.

.   .   .   .

"If beggers haunt thee, let thy servants drive them away, thou withdrawing out of ear-shot.

". . . Drink the breath of wholesome infants as often as

thou conveniently canst,—it is good for thy purpose; also the breath of buxom maids, if thou mayest without undue disturbance of the flesh, drink it as a morning-draught, as medicine; also the breath of cows as they return from rich pasture at eventide.[47]

That these precepts are ironic is evident on the face of them. The idea that a "decent degree of good and kindness" is valuable because it brings one "a slight pleasurable sense" is evidence enough that benevolence is not to be cultivated for its own sake; and the comparison of the breath of "wholesome infants" and "buxom maids" with that of cows returning from pasture, though indicative of a certain scientific acumen in the classification of phenomena, is also proof positive of a lack of awareness of human values. All the precepts form a remarkable inversion of the Christian ideas that a man may save his life by losing it, or that there is any value in laying down one's life for his friend. Indeed, one should lay down his friend's life for himself, and one ends up, as Septimius finds out too late, by losing his life through attempting to save it.

Hawthorne himself has given away the purpose of this recipe for longevity in one of the preliminary drafts for the romance: "Certain conditions are required by this recipe, the general tendency of which is, to contract a man within himself, estrange him from his fellows and all the earnest struggle of humanity, cut off the foliage of his affections &c. Perhaps the recipe shall be given in a letter to the young man from his uncle, written in a quaint style, with moral precepts, indicating egotism under the guise of a philosophy of restrained passions."[48] In the romance as it now exists the recipe is not given Septimius by his uncle; but this is the only real change in development from the sketch to the story. The idea of what the precepts are symbolic of—a high type of egotism—remains unchanged.

This basic irony is emphasized still further by Septimius' discussion of what he will do with his eternal life when once he is assured of it.[49] On a walk one day with Sibyl Dacy, he tells her of his plans in his future existence. He will, quite literally, try to live all possible lives, to experience all things. Nothing human will be foreign to him, even though to gain this desirable end of knowing all human experience he has estranged himself from it. The paradox does not seem to bother him. He will travel, rule, cure the evils of mankind, play and devote himself to pastimes, learn deep philosophies, study, and enjoy the fruits of posterity which he as ruler has provided for himself, all of these things to be done in succession over one-hundred-year periods. He will even be wicked for a century, in order to learn by experience what a wicked man feels, for he, like Faust, would learn everything through doing it. Though he would be wicked himself, however, he wishes Sibyl to remain "good and pure" in order to be the means for his redemption. The irony is magnificent.

At the conclusion of his rapturous monologue, Sibyl asks him if he would never wish to sleep, if only for a few centuries. He denies that he would ever want to rest, and is incapable of conceiving that man would ever actually desire repose. The ironic contrast in the idea here is again generally very clear. Septimius, like the old people whom Dr. Heidegger has delusively rejuvenated, has no conception of any happiness not exclusively related to the joys of earth, and can conceive neither of the higher joys of eternity nor even of the fact that earthly pleasures might grow stale. He does not have the wisdom of Faust, who sells his soul to the Devil knowing full well that the Devil's offer is a delusion, that there will never in the nature of things be a moment of temporal happiness to which he can honestly say "*Verweile doch, du bist so schön.*"

When Richard Henry Stoddard sent Hawthorne a copy of his just-finished long poem *The King's Bell* in 1863, Hawthorne was hard at work on the composition of *Septimius Felton. The King's Bell* bears a close resemblance to *Septimius Felton* in meaning, though it is considerably more conventional in presentation. The hero of *The King's Bell*, a young king named "Felix," is not given an elixir of life but is given a similar gift in the expectation of all possible earthly happiness. He is young, wealthy, and a king, and should have, if anyone ever does, the positive assurance of unlimited temporal happiness. One of the first acts of his reign is to mount a bell in his castle which he plans to ring whenever he is happy, but as he goes through life in an honorable and apparently fortunate manner, he is never able to find one moment which is blissful enough to justify the ringing of the bell. He becomes initiated into the knowledge that earthly joy is in its nature imperfect sorrow, and finds no perfect happiness in fame, in marriage, in military glory, in the ideal of being a just ruler, or in any of the more ephemeral human pleasures of the senses. His name, Felix, the happy or the fortunate one, which at the beginning of his reign was a name auspicious of happiness, becomes constantly more ironic. Yet we discover that Felix really has found that true happiness, which is just the opposite of that happiness which Septimius Felton desires, can be found in death, and that his name is not really ironic at all. Symbolic of his final wisdom is the concluding episode of the poem, where he at last rings the bell and dies.

This short summary of Stoddard's work shows how closely related it is thematically to several of the themes handled by Hawthorne. Indeed, the whole image of the bell at the end of the poem, paradoxically tolling joyously, is almost parallel to the end of Hawthorne's much earlier tale "The Wedding Knell." The whole parabolic tone of the poem is Hawthornean in quality, and its dominant themes, the passing of earthly joy and the insufficiency of earthly happiness, are ones which were dear to Hawthorne's heart.

After reading the poem, Hawthorne sent a letter of thanks to Stoddard, in which he mused upon the meaning of Felix's ringing the bell. "I think Felix might have rung the bell once in his lifetime, and once again at the moment of death," he begins, but then characteristically qualifies his statement: "Yet you may be right. I have been a happy man, and yet I do not remember any one moment of such happy conspiring that I could have rung a joy-bell at it."[50] Hawthorne's statement here is almost the same as Faust's in its realization of the impossibility of complete earthly happiness. It is diametrically opposed to the attitude of Septimius Felton.

Nevertheless, Septimius himself, though shown up as foolish and misguided, is not condemned so thoroughly as are the elderly epicures whom Dr. Heidegger rejuvenated. Septimius has tried to surpass the limits of human existence for reasons which are more profound and more justifiable than the mere satisfaction of sensual experience. He had hoped to learn, to understand, to discover the meaning of life, and, since he could not hope to do this in one lifetime, had attempted to live forever. He, like Aylmer, lacked the higher wisdom which would have seen that the quest itself was foolish, that no matter how long his life lasted he would see only through a glass darkly; but his effort itself is not wholly to be condemned, though it results in failure. His fate is very close to that of Aylmer, that is, if we assume that Hawthorne had intended to let the ending in the published version of *Septimius Felton* stand. Both men, in pursuit of a high yet perverse ideal, sacrifice out of the highest motives the persons who are dearest to them. The high ideals at which Septimius has aimed are to be regarded with pity rather than with contempt. Septimius has not realized that there are other goods than those of this earth, and has failed to understand that for him, as for every man, there is never world enough or time.

The Dolliver Romance, which is much less complete than *Septimius Felton*, continues this probing of the motives of the searcher after the elixir of life still more profoundly. There is no real evidence to enable us to conjecture even remotely how the tale would have been written as far as the plot is concerned, but it is easy to see from the one complete chapter which we have that the most striking difference between this romance and its predecessor lies in the deeper sympathy with which Dr. Dolliver is handled. For Dr. Dolliver has no possible reason of his own to live except for love of another, his granddaughter Pansie. He drinks the elixir of youth and begins his rejuvenation for completely unselfish purposes, and in so doing places himself in a rather profoundly paradoxical position. If he is committing a grave sin he is certainly doing so for the best of motives, and it is difficult to see, with Hawthorne's statement of the case, an old man with a completely dependent granddaughter who is suddenly given the means to provide for her, what else he could have done. Had he decided to let himself die rather than drink the water of youth which would enable him to provide for Pansie's welfare he would have been guilty of far greater selfishness than he was guilty of by actually drinking the elixir.

Hawthorne deliberately seems to be setting the stage for a very ambiguous and profound searching of the moral problem of just when what might appear to be selfishness is in actuality so, and when it is justified by service to another. Certainly Dr. Dolliver's ideal of service is a much higher one than that selfish one by which Septimius is forced to live in order to discover the recipe for eternal life. In a very real sense, Dr. Dolliver is laying down his life for another by refusing the gift of eternity to take what he knows are the lesser satisfactions of earthly life, by sacrificing his own best interest for the good of a young child for whose care he is not directly responsible, who has never asked him to sacrifice himself for her, and whose welfare will in no way promote his own.

To make this statement more complicated, Hawthorne, through the image of Dr. Dolliver's eyes, which, like Chillingworth's, take on an unearthly glow as he commits what is apparently a sin, suggests that there is some other way in which he should have behaved. What this other way is, if indeed it actually exists, it is useless to conjecture. But however the plot of the tale might have developed, it is clear that the theme of the search for the elixir of youth and its use when once found has been conceived in a much more complex and subtle way than ever before.

Without too much oversimplification, it might well be said that the progress of Hawthorne's career in general follows the pattern I have suggested in particular for the development of the theme of immortality, that is, toward ever greater ambiguity and sophistication. Harry Levin has remarked that "Fiction, for Hawthorne, is always the working-out of an improbable hypothesis. What would happen if—?",[51] and one might well suggest that Hawthorne's literary development is coincidental with the skill with which he can ask and answer this question.

At times, notably in his earlier tales, the forming of the subjunctive plot, the placing together of improbable characters in an improbable situation, is done by means of some bizarre occurrence which may speak truth about some profound human situation. One of his earliest tales, "The Hollow of the Three Hills," composed probably before 1825, for example, revolves around a young girl's visiting a witch in order to find out the effect of her crime upon those dear to her. More common, however, in the earlier tales, is the establishment of some central thematic statement of which two separate points of view can be shown.

In "The Maypole of Merry Mount," written probably in 1828 or 1829, this can be seen very clearly. The story revolves around the Puritan raid upon Mt. Wollaston, and the carrying off of the revelers to the haunts of the godly. Hawthorne, in this tale, has falsified history somewhat to make the Puritan raid take place when a marriage ceremony is being performed at Merry Mount. To add to the symbolic contrast, this wedding ceremony is being celebrated beneath a Maypole, which is the symbol of the Merry Mount colony. That Hawthorne uses the Maypole here as a phallic symbol is doubtful; he does, nevertheless, very nicely show the essential falsity of the Merry Mount society by opposing its values to the values of the true lovers, by symbolically opposing the Maypole to the Lord and Lady of the May, pleasure (though not necessarily licentiousness) to love. When the Puritans attack Merry Mount, the Maypole symbol is very pointedly amplified, for the Puritans have their own Maypole, as Hawthorne tells us, the whipping post. When Endicott cuts down the Maypole, symbolically destroying the existential principle of Merry Mount, he regrets that he has not left it standing so that he could give each of the captives another dance around it. He concludes grimly that, "It would have served rarely for a whipping-post."[52]

This tale has often, and I think correctly, been interpreted as a statement of a golden mean between two fanatical extremes, the two lovers, Edith and Edgar, being the human mean between the extremes of Puritanism and Merry Mount, symbolically considered. This is perhaps too patly shown at the end of the story, when Endicott himself throws a wreath of roses over the heads of the two young lovers, symbolically uniting in them the virtues of both Puritans and Merry Mounters. For our purpose, however, the most significant aspect of the tale is the image of the Maypole, which is made to do double duty, and to signify two precisely opposite characteristics. In later tales, when Hawthorne grows more sure of his medium, he will not need to use two symbols for two opposed purposes, but will combine them into one. He will be able to suggest, through the term Maypole, both the meaning connected with it by the Puritans and by the denizens of Mt. Wollaston.

Further development in the use of this symbolic technique may be seen in "The Shaker Bridal," written probably in 1831. This second of the marriage group in Hawthorne's tales depends also on a duality of meanings, the inherent paradox in the idea of matrimony in a celibate society. This matrimony, like the Merry Mounters' view of marriage, is an illusory one, and is indeed the very opposite of matrimony as it is normally understood. To make the irony more striking, the marriage is made a hollow mockery of what the true marriage of Adam and Martha should have been, had they acted wisely. The story does not really oppose the ideal of celibacy to that of matrimony, but rather discusses marriage through the images of two types of perversion, metaphorically shown by the paradoxical celibate marriage in a Shaker community and the particular perversion of the matrimonial ideal in Adam's own case. A nun is supposedly a bride of Christ, not a celibate sister of her earthly lover. Hawthorne has, however, in this story managed to show the irony of this "marriage" through a series of symbolic contrasts, basically opposing matrimony to celibacy, all of which are tied together in the symbol of marriage. He does not any longer need two symbolic marriages as he had earlier needed two Maypoles, in order to show opposite qualities.

In a slightly later tale, "The Wedding Knell" (1835), Hawthorne again uses the device of polarities resolved within a single symbol. The basic symbol of the story, as in "The Shaker Bridal," is the symbol of marriage. The irony in this tale is that there is now no question of a real marriage for either Mrs. Dabney or John Ellenwood. To pretend that such a marriage is a "real" marriage, as Mrs. Dabney is bent on doing, is almost as foolish as to pretend with the Merry Mounters that there is no such thing as sorrow. In this tale Mrs. Dabney is apparently the less aware of the futility of any such marriage, and it is easy to interpret John Ellenwood as a kind of *deus ex machina* who restores her to a rational view of the real state of human affairs.

Such a reading, however, is too simplistic, and ignores the fact that if Mrs. Dabney has been vain, John Ellenwood has been vindictive. Like Jervayse Helwyse, despair has maddened him. The resolution of the tale comes not only when Mrs. Dabney realizes that her life is gone in "vanity and emptiness," but when John Ellenwood comes to understand that he has, by his cruelty, committed, if anything, a worse crime. He comes to the understanding that the despair of a life spent in useless waiting has almost completely embittered him, and concludes, like Roderick Elliston, by asking his wife's forgiveness.[53] Instead of wedding for time, the two old people wed, as they say, for Eternity, and thus restore some dignity to what otherwise would have been a hollow mockery. For theirs is a true marriage, though true to a different law than most marriages, and its truth is enhanced, rather than destroyed, by our knowledge that for them in heaven, as for each on earth, there will be no bride.

Hawthorne was not, however, content to rest with symbols which showed only the opposite intellectual sides of a given point of view. He was constantly in quest of a more subtle symbolic structure than this rather mechanical development in terms of opposites could give him. Even in some of his earlier stories this investigation of symbols in terms of opposites develops into something quite different. "The Gentle Boy," written in 1828 or 1829, is a case in point. In this story the central symbol is the Gentle Boy himself, the Quaker waif Ilbrahim who is at once a victim of religious fanaticism in its most violent forms, enthusiasm and persecution.

It is easy to read this tale as a study of a boy who in some way represents a right course of action, placed in opposition to two distinct fanaticisms, symbolically depicted in his Quaker mother and the society of his Puritan foster-parents. Something of this is certainly present in the tale. The Quakers and Puritans are both representatives of fanaticisms which Ilbrahim himself and his foster parents, Tobias and Dorothy Pearson, avoid. Dorothy and Tobias Pearson, by their befriending of the outcast Ilbrahim, perform a moral action which is in singular contrast to that of their Christian brethren on either side—Catherine, the frenzied Quaker prophetess who is the boy's real mother, and the intolerant Puritans, aptly symbolized by the boy whom Ilbrahim has befriended who takes the part of his enemies against him.[54] Probably the basic, and certainly one of the most important, aspects of this complex tale lies in the symbolic contrast of Tobias and Dorothy Pearson with the unnatural fanaticism of Ilbrahim's mother on the one hand and the intolerance of the Puritans on the other.

It is only too clear that we should all act like the Pearsons and avoid the fanaticisms of either extreme. In actual fact, however, such a course is impossible, and Hawthorne shows its impossibility through the attitudes of the various other characters toward Ilbrahim, the Gentle Boy, an outcast at once from his parents and from society. By means of their reactions to this enigmatic boy, Hawthorne is able to show not only the extremes of behavior in the Puritans and the Quakers, but various shadings in between in the persons of the Gentle Boy himself, of his foster-parents Dorothy and Tobias Pearson, and of his mother, Catherine, and, at the same time, the impossibility of right conduct in this sorry world.

Certainly the point of view represented by the Pearsons and Ilbrahim is the Christian, the noble, the forgiving spirit, which results in Ilbrahim's being beaten by the Puritan children, and in the Pearsons' being ostracized by the godly members of the community in which they live. Lest we should take the sentimental view that time heals all things, or that to know all is to forgive all, Hawthorne reminds us of the edifying result on the Puritan settlement of Catherine's presence there, in one of the most searing denunciations ever penned of the state of things as they are.

As if Ilbrahim's sweetness yet lingered round his ashes; as if his gentle spirit came down from heaven to teach his parent a true religion, her fierce and vindictive nature was softened by the same griefs which had once irritated it. When the course of years had made the features of the unobtrusive mourner familiar in the settlement, she became a subject of not deep, but general, interest; a being on whom the otherwise superfluous sympathies of all might be bestowed. Every one spoke of her with that degree of pity which it is pleasant to experience; every one was ready to do her the little kindnesses which are not costly, yet manifest good will; and when at last she died, a long train of her once bitter persecutors followed her, with decent sadness and tears that were not painful, to her place by Ilbrahim's green and sunken grave.[55]

In this tale, Hawthorne has for the first time stumbled upon a method of elaboration of his symbolic technique which became constantly more important to him. He has discovered that a given central symbol can be used in more than one way. In "The Gentle Boy," to oversimplify a bit, Ilbrahim was used symbolically in two ways. Basically he was used as a foil for all the various characters in order to show their separate reactions to his plight. Ethically, the attitude of the Pearsons toward him was the most moral and noble, an example of the *via media* between two types of extremism, the fanaticism of the Quakers and the intolerance of the Puritans.

At the same time, Ilbrahim was used as the focal point for a related, yet quite different theme, which one might paraphrase as the effect of crime on the community. This tale is an examination of the regenerative power of sin, a theme which fascinated Hawthorne later in *The Scarlet Letter, The House of the Seven Gables*, and most of all in *The Marble Faun*. For in "The Gentle Boy," as in these latter tales, the question is raised of the educative effects of sin, in this story shown through examination of the beneficent effect upon the community of their feeling of responsibility for Ilbrahim's death.

Both these themes, though, unite in the symbolic personage of Ilbrahim, who is the focal point of the story. As in "My Kinsman, Major Molyneux," which was composed at almost exactly the same time, the central symbol is a human being, and just what he himself means is uncertain. The symbolic importance of Ilbrahim, as the symbolic importance of Major Molyneux, is not so much what he himself *is* as what he *is understood to be*. Ilbrahim and Major Molyneux are important for their effects on other characters, not for what they themselves stand for or represent. In these tales, in short, the central image is important not primarily in and for itself, but rather in the eyes of those who behold it. Symbolic meaning lies not in the symbolic object itself, but in the perception of meaning in the object by others. Ilbrahim, then, is important symbolically in two ways. First, he is the focal point of two distinct thematic lines of development. Second, his symbolic meaning is not expressed by means of what he himself does or is, but rather by others' perceptions of symbolic meaning in him and in his fate.

This complexity in symbolism becomes constantly more subtle, reaching what is probably its high point in one of Hawthorne's latest short tales, "Rappaccini's Daughter," probably written in the autumn of 1844, and certainly not before the autumn of 1842.[56] The great problem in interpreting this tale has always been to discover just who the villain in it is. Is Beatrice in some way at fault, or is Rappaccini? What about Giovanni and Baglioni? The story is apparently one of good and evil, and it is tempting to find in Rappaccini's garden a type of an inverse Eden, Eden after the Fall, if you will. The mysterious purple shrub is a kind of inverse tree of knowledge, Rappaccini a type of post-lapsarian Adam, and Beatrice in some paradoxical way both a pure and a corrupted Eve. Her name suggests Dante's ideal woman, while her nature suggests poison. Yet if she is evil, Giovanni, her disillusioned lover, though conventionally moral is not really good. And, conversely, if Beatrice is good, Giovanni's actions seem more conventional than evil. A similar mystery is found if one asks what the story is really about. Is the focus of the tale on Rappaccini himself, the diabolical scientist who sacrifices his daughter to his love of knowledge, or is it rather on Giovanni, whose love for Beatrice is weighed in the balance and found wanting?

R. R. Male, Jr., has pointed out that in actual fact both of these interpretations of the tale are valid. On the more literally apparent level, Beatrice is poisonous and Giovanni is perfectly justified in forsaking her. On another level, however, Beatrice is a type of what Male sees as a religious ideal, and Baglioni, *not* Rappaccini, is the evil one, the empiric rationalist who destroys Giovanni's faith in what appears logically to be an absurd and unreal ideal. The story on this level might be read

as a statement of the Tertullian paradox, *Credo quia ineptum.*
Giovanni should, according to this reading, take Beatrice's
beauties on faith, rather than succumbing to the skepticism of
Baglioni. The important point in Male's interpretation of the
story, though, is not which of these two apparently opposite
interpretations is the correct one—and quotations can be bandied
about on either side—but the fact that both exist simultaneously
in the tale, that both interplay with each other, and that both are
diametrically opposed.

In the story two themes move in direct opposition to each
other, but through the actions of the same characters. There are,
exclusive of Beatrice, who, like the Gentle Boy is important
primarily as a symbolic statement of experience upon which the
other characters act, three major characters in the story: Rappaccini, Baglioni, and Giovanni. If the tale is an exploration of a
man's sacrificing the human values of sympathy and love to a
cold love of knowledge, then Rappaccini is the villain, Giovanni
his deluded dupe, and Baglioni the heroic savior. If, on the
other hand, the story is an exploration of the question of the
validity of knowledge, told in terms of two kinds of perception—
faith and empirical science—Rappaccini is in a sense the hero
of the tale, and Giovanni is deluded by the blasphemous skepticism of Baglioni. But the tale is not an "either-or" statement. It
is an exploration of both these problems simultaneously, and,
more significantly, *through only one plot line.* Given one plot
involving the interaction of three characters, two practically
opposite interpretations are not only possible but actually exist
simultaneously within the tale, producing, as Male puts it, "a
rich irony which our prosaic commentary can but clumsily
indicate."[57]

What has happened in this tale is that Hawthorne has completely removed any possibility of a simple interpretation on the
basis of identification with a character of which he apparently
approves. Whatever meaning the tale possesses is a meaning in
terms of our perception of the interaction of two completely
opposite viewpoints upon an apparently fantastic reality. The
world of Rappaccini's garden is given us by Hawthorne, and,
like the snake in Roderick Elliston's bosom, we must accept it

as at least fictionally true. But our perception of reality in terms of this world cannot be in the perception of what meaning lies behind it, but rather in the fact that two completely opposite interpretations of this reality are possible. Although the world of Rappaccini's garden is paradoxical, its paradoxicality itself is what Hawthorne insists upon, not the reconciliation of apparently opposite aspects of it.

The same subtlety in the use of symbols is basic to *The Scarlet Letter*, which bears a very close resemblance to "Rappaccini's Daughter." In *The Scarlet Letter* again are three individuals who interact with each other through their perception into the meaning of the mysterious bond which unites them, the crime of adultery symbolized by the letter which Hester Prynne must wear on her bosom. Most of the literally hundreds of discussions of the novel, like the fewer discussions of "Rappaccini's Daughter," attempt to solve the meaning of the fate of Hester Prynne in terms of some kind of moral justification. Were Hester Prynne and Arthur Dimmesdale justified, or were they not, in their commission of what is conventionally considered a sin? Is it possible to arrange the three characters into some hierarchy in terms of their sinfulness, and if so, how does one go about it? Do Hester and Arthur Dimmesdale ever really repent of their crime, and, if they do, are they saved or damned? Has Hester's sin a regenerative effect or has it not?

All these questions legitimately arise out of any discussion of *The Scarlet Letter*, and practically any interpretation of the romance can be justified on the basis of passages which occur within it. This is, in my opinion, indicative of only one thing, that Hawthorne's purpose in writing the tale was not to state a moral point, but rather to show the incompleteness of any moral reading of the problems in the tale. Hawthorne is not so much concerned with showing whether or not Hester is saved or damned as with showing that on the basis of the facts we have at our disposal no ultimate justification or condemnation of Hester's and Dimmesdale's conduct is possible.

The various ethical readings of the novel, all of which are extremely plausible and quite different, indicate to me the impossibility of any ethical interpretation of the tale. When Hawthorne said of *The Scarlet Letter* that it was a hell-fired story, I suggest that he did not mean that its ethic was diabolically inspired, but—what is really much more depressing to those critics who are too much at home in Zion—that there is no ethical resolution to the story at all. If anything, the book is an even-tempered denial of the sufficiency of an ethical interpretation of reality.

In *The Scarlet Letter* Hawthorne uses ethical ideas as philosophical counters and, after playing with them, good-humoredly discards them all. The reality behind the apparent sin of Hester and Dimmesdale can be understood only in terms of its effects upon the three characters themselves, and upon society in general. But the psychological validity of the effect of sin on the various characters, say, for example, in diabolizing Chillingworth, has no metaphysical reality. Because Chillingworth is (or is not) diabolized, because Hester is (or is not) ennobled by adultery, because Dimmesdale does (or does not) come to the realization that repentance brings salvation, has nothing at all to do with Sin in general. Sin, as Young Goodman Brown discovered, is a fact of human experience, yet in its nature is unknowable. It can be discussed only in regard to its effects upon human beings and their relationships with each other.

Hawthorne's final and most complex statement of the impossibility of precise knowledge of any aspect of human experience comes in his last, consistently underrated romance, *The Marble Faun.* As in the various discussions of *The Scarlet Letter,* critical interpretations of this romance have raged around the interpretation of an ethical problem, in this case the doctrine of the Fortunate Fall. Are Miriam and Donatello justified? Is Hilda representative of a moral type of spotless purity or is she rather a prudish and hypocritical perpetrator of the Unpardonable Sin? Does Hawthorne mean to show through the character of Donatello that innocence is impossible in the modern world, and that ancient times were really better, the symbolic evidence of Rome to the contrary? And what does he have to say about the effect of sin on those who are not directly concerned with it: in Donatello's fall are we damnéd all?

Again, as we have learned to expect, all the ethical questions center on the mythical Donatello, whose nature, like his ears, remains enigmatic to the last. He commits, like Hester Prynne, what society considers a crime, though whether it is really one in any terms of ultimate truth remains as uncertain at the end of the book as it was the instant the crime was committed. The problem explored in the book is again not an ethical one nor a metaphysical one but rather a psychological one, though it is explored in metaphysical and ethical terms. All we ever discover about ultimate reality in *The Marble Faun* is that certain characters, when confronted with a fact of experience, interpret it in a certain way. When Hilda is faced by the fact that Miriam has been partially responsible for what she considers a crime, her innocence, at least of the knowledge of evil, is destroyed. Hawthorne comments quasi-moralistically that "Every crime destroys more Edens than our own!"[58] This is a statement, however, of a psychological, not of a metaphysical fact. Kenyon's Eden is not destroyed at all by the revelation of Miriam's crime, even though he is just as untainted with actual guilt as Hilda is.

Similarly, the various statements about whether or not the Romance of Monte Beni re-enacts the Fall of Man, and whether Man's Fall is a vehicle for redemption, are important only as psychological statements on the part of the various characters who make them. Furthermore, Hawthorne does not suggest that some characters have more enlightened opinions than others, though the sympathies of readers today (unlike those of readers of fifty years ago) are on the side of Miriam rather than Hilda. In *The Marble Faun* we are introduced into a quite typical, though somewhat more elaborate than usual, Hawthornean world which we must accept without question. In this world is an impossible and bizarre symbol, a modern-day faun, emblematic of some aspect of human experience which is never more precisely explained. The characters in the romance become involved in a paradoxical crime which this supposedly virtuous symbol commits, and from the perception of which they attempt to deduce its moral effect on him. Miriam decides that Donatello's fall opens the way to a higher existence; Hilda denies this; Kenyon, who is, like Hawthorne, an artist, ponders both interpretations and finds neither one satisfactory; and Donatello, in keeping with his symbolic forerunners, is uncompromisingly silent, though he, if anyone, is in the only position to know the truth.

Although *The Marble Faun* appears at first glance to be an ethical study, in actual fact it is nothing of the kind. Hawthorne will not attempt to justify the ways of God to man. Such an attempt is not only vain but futile, for God's purposes are inscrutable, and man's accidents interpretable only in human terms.

The Marble Faun has brought us by a commodius vicus of recirculation back through the development of Hawthorne's art. The symbolic structure has been elaborated—perhaps overelaborated—to an almost incredible degree. On the other hand, the principle behind this elaboration is one which Hawthorne had followed from his earliest artistic career, the belief that objective reality is at last explicable only in terms of its subjective effects, that these effects are often paradoxical and never clear, that unity can ultimately be understood only through the infinite proliferation of detail.

Hawthorne and the Comic Spirit

THERE IS CERTAINLY little place for the comic spirit in the Hawthornean world which Van Wyck Brooks sees as "a new creation. . . . All very simple, . . . simple as the brightly colored leaves that drift over a sedgy stream, only that too often, before one's eyes, the stream sang its way out of the meadow and carried its bright burden into the forest, where all grew dark and baleful."[1] This has been the traditional view of Hawthorne's world, but there is contrary evidence.

One very good example of critical unwillingness to face up squarely to the problem of Hawthorne's humor may well stand for all. The so-called "Dofobs Edition" of Hawthorne's love letters, while not easily accessible, has been available since 1907, before most of the modern biographies were written.[2] This edition contains the famous "haunted chamber" letter to Sophia which is generally quoted as proof positive that Hawthorne was a gloomy, maladjusted recluse, and the letter seems, indeed, to justify such a conclusion, on the face of it.

> Here sits thy husband in his old accustomed chamber, where he used to sit in years gone by, before his soul became acquainted with thine. Here I have written many tales—many that have been burned to ashes—many that doubtless deserved the same fate. This deserves to be called a haunted chamber, for thousands upon thousand of visions have appeared to me in it: and some few of them have become visible to the world. If ever I should have a biographer he ought to make great mention of this chamber in my memoirs, because so much of my lonely youth was wasted here, and here my mind and character were formed; and here I have been glad and hopeful, and here I have

been despondent; and here I sat a long, long time, waiting
for the world to know me, and sometimes wondering why
it did not know me sooner, or whether it would ever know
me at all—at least, till I were in my grave.[3]

There is, however, another side to the denizen of the haunted
chamber, a side which it is too easy to ignore. For Hawthorne
wrote another letter about his life in this chamber to his
fiancée, a letter as different from the above as one letter can
be from another, although it begins in the same manner.

Here is thy husband in his old chamber, where he produced
these stupendous works of fiction, which have since im-
pressed the Universe with wonderment and awe! To this
chamber, doubtless, in all succeeding ages, pilgrims will
come to pay their tribute of reverence;—they will put off
their shoes at the threshold, for fear of desecrating the
tattered old carpet. "There" they will exclaim, "is the very
bed in which he slumbered, and where he was visited
by those ethereal visions, which he afterward fixed forever
in glowing words! There is the washstand, at which this
exalted personage cleansed himself from the stains of earth,
and rendered his outward man a fitting exponent of the
pure soul within. There, in its mahogany frame, is the
dressing-glass, which reflected that noble brow, those
hyacinthine locks, that mouth, bright with smiles, or
tremulous with feeling, that flashing or melting eye, that—
in short, every item of the magnanimous phiz of this unex-
ampled man! There is the pine table—there the old flag-
bottomed chair—in which he sat, and at which he scribbled,
during his agonies of inspiration! There is the old chest
of drawers, in which he kept what shirts a poor author may
be supposed to have possessed! There is the closet, in which
was reposited his threadbare suit of black! There is the
wornout shoe-brush with which this polished writer polished
his boots. There is—but I believe this will be pretty much all;
—so here I close the catalogue.[4]

It is almost as if Hawthorne had stumbled into a guided tour of
the House of the Seven Gables!

It is not my purpose here to attempt to answer the violently contested question of whether or not Hawthorne *was* in reality a maladjusted and pathologically shy and morbid individual. But I do think it is significant that only two of all Hawthorne's biographers have quoted this second letter or even hinted at its existence, and Hawthorne's critics to the best of my knowledge have ignored it as well.[5] It seems to me that the statement of any case for Hawthorne's pathological mental state or, more to my purposes, of his high seriousness, should not ignore what are apparently facts to the contrary. One of the invaluable services which modern scholarship has done is to show that Hawthorne was a most complex person and a most subtle artist. I think there is very little need for a further discussion of Hawthorne as a tragic writer, since R. H. Fogle, H. H. Waggoner, and R. R. Male, Jr. have studied this aspect of his art at length.[6] Hawthorne as a comic writer, however, has received somewhat too little attention.

The two "haunted chamber" letters quoted above bring us to the central problem of Hawthorne's comic spirit. There is no real way to tell, other than by consulting our preconceptions, which of these apparently opposite statements represents the "real" Hawthorne. We must, for lack of any other evidence, assume that both are at least subjectively true, that each represents a genuine Hawthornean attitude toward a "fact," his long apprenticeship as a writer. To assume that he wrote the second letter as a kind of *jeu d'esprit* or camouflage for his wounded psyche is tempting but unverifiable. Perhaps the reverse is true. No one has discussed seriously the plausible suggestion that Hawthorne was *not* a Byronic spirit who laughed to keep from weeping; indeed, it is likely that weeping and laughing were both true for him, that he could go to the house of feasting with all the ease with which he could go to the house of mourning and feel at home in either.

Perhaps his use of humor is analogous to his complex use of symbolism discussed in the last chapter, as another, non-tragic method of explaining a complex reality. It is my contention that Hawthorne discovered Reality to be constantly more ambiguous, inexplicable in terms of itself and only limitedly understandable in terms of its effects. As I have suggested earlier, the multiplication of detail was Hawthorne's only answer to the vexing yet compelling problem of how to know anything of ultimate Reality. Hawthorne's view of tragedy and comedy is analogous to his view of the function of symbol within his tales. That is, tragedy and comedy are two distinct points of view in terms of which a given event may be interpreted; each one is valid and to some extent dependent upon the other.

Most discussions of tragedy begin with the elementary statement that tragedy is not tragic by virtue of its subject matter. Because someone dies in a drama is no reason to assume that the drama is necessarily tragedy—it may be melodrama, or, more likely, it may be pathos. Tragedy is only possible when the tragic hero—or tragic victim, if you prefer—becomes in some way conscious of the meaning of his tragic fate. When Othello comes to a full realization of the villainy of Iago, this is the moment of tragedy, not the moment when Othello commits suicide. Othello's suicide itself is not tragic, but the pathetic result of his final tragic awareness. Similarly, when someone is run over by a streetcar this is not necessarily tragedy, whatever the newspapers may call it. It is sad and terrible, but it carries no necessary perception of the meaning of one's fate with it; it is not tragedy but pathos. Critics of Hawthorne's tragedy frequently seem to confuse the often unhappy results of the tales with a tragic awareness on the part of the characters. Darrel Abel has taken exception to this view with a good deal of justice. He defines tragedy as the showing of "greatness destroyed," where pathos "is the effect of anything which shows feebleness frustrated." Given this definition he concludes that "Most of Hawthorne's tales show evil thus in a pathetic, not tragic aspect. Nevertheless, a pathetic story has its share of poignancy for anyone skilled in envisioning possibilities—in observing the discrepancy between a man's dream of what might be, and his perception of what is, his own lot."[7]

If one may expand Abel's definition, what he seems to mean is that the effect of sadness and waste which we perceive in Hawthorne's "tragic" tales comes not through our perception of the tragic awareness on the part of the hero but through our realization that the world is too strong for the limited characters which appear. This is actually fairly close to the orthodox view of comedy, at least as a serious art. For comedy should not correctly be defined as an art form which makes us laugh. Comedy may make us laugh, but then again it may not, and the definition in any case mistakes means for ends. Comedy is a mode of perceiving Reality in which the comic victims are seen to deviate from some accepted standard, it may be with pathetic results. Similarly, Hawthorne's "tragic" characters deviate from an acceptable standard, again with pathetic results. In short, tragedy and comedy for Hawthorne are two distinct modes of apprehending experience, and not results of the plots of his tale.

As an example of a pathetic use of comedy which is roughly contemporaneous with Hawthorne, let us take George Meredith. Meredith stoutly declares that *The Ordeal of Richard Feverel* is a comic novel. If we take his statement at face value, we are forced to assume that the novel is in some way a comedy in its action, not in its results, and that its comicality is completely divorced from humor. No one would pretend that the end of the novel, with Lucy dead, Richard's happiness destroyed, and Sir Austin still prating about his "system" is at all funny. Yet Meredith insists that the novel is a comic one. Whatever comedy there is, then, must be in the attitudes of the characters themselves which bring about the catastrophic ending of the story, not in the ending itself. Comedy, for Meredith, is an attitude toward experience which may, as in *Evan Harrington*, fall within the limits of the humorous or, as in *Richard Feverel*, definitely does not. This attitude toward comedy is very similar to Hawthorne's. For Hawthorne assumes that tragedy and comedy are both means of *apprehending* reality, not means of stating the results of an individual's contact with it. Comedy is just as serious for him as tragedy, capable of as profound insights, and productive of about the same results. This is not to suggest, of course, that "comedy" and "humor" are necessarily divorced for Hawthorne, or that his comic vision is somehow or other not funny. Such is rather obviously not the case. What I do mean to suggest, however, is that Hawthorne's humor, even at its broadest, almost always serves a serious purpose.

Basic to Hawthorne's comic vision, it seems to me, is an

unerring sense of the ludicrous, especially of the humor inherent in the difference between man's noble pretentions and often rather feeble performance. Hawthorne could see only too well how foolish people are by virtue of their very humanity, and the most foolish when the most sober. Horatio Bridge remembers Hawthorne as delighting in blowing the horn at five o'clock in the morning at Brook Farm, "much to the discomfort of the drowsy members of the family,"[8] in order to get the sluggards to rise and further the progress of the human race. And everyone knows Hawthorne's reference to Margaret Fuller's gift to the Brook Farm community—an unmanageable cow—as the "transcendental heifer." James T. Fields tells that Hawthorne had "an inexhaustible store of amusing anecdotes to relate of people and things he had observed on the road," though he does not give any examples of these anecdotes. He does tell, however, one story which was a favorite with Hawthorne, and the humor of which depends upon the ludicrousness of the party concerned. "I once told him of a young woman who brought in a manuscript, and said, as she placed it in my hands, 'I don't know what to do with myself sometimes, I'm so filled with *mammoth thoughts*'."[9]

On the most elementary level, Hawthorne's sense of the ludicrous may be seen in his fondness of playing with words. The whole conclusion of one of his earlier tales depends upon a rather labored word-play. "The Devil in Manuscript," probably composed in 1834, although possibly as early as 1825, ends with an expanded and rather bad verbal quibble. Oberon, the frustrated and ignored author, has burned up his manuscripts only to find that the flames from the fire have set the roofs of the town ablaze. He breaks into a triumphantly ironic paean of artistic self-vindication: "'My tales!' cried Oberon. 'The chimney! The roof! The Fiend has gone forth by night, and startled thousands in fear and wonder from their beds! Here I stand,—a triumphant author! Huzza! Huzza! My brain has set the town on fire! Huzza!'"[10]

The scholar is likely to find this type of humor somewhat distressing, but Hawthorne seemed to like it. All the various solemnly proferred meanings of the "A" in *The Scarlet Letter* are little more than quibbles, though used with a serious purpose.

Even as an older and presumably wiser man Hawthorne used them as vehicles for his own amusement. In the "Consular Experiences" section of *Our Old Home* he reflects on the visits to his chambers of "a young English friend, a scholar and a literary amateur," who became one of his intimates. Hawthorne muses, "It would gratify my cherished remembrance of this dear friend, if I could manage, without offending him, or letting the public know it, to introduce his name upon my page. Bright was the illumination of my dusky little apartment, as often as he made his appearance there!"[11] The friend was, of course, Henry Bright, and the pun was evidently a source of enjoyment.

The significance of these quibbles lies not so much in themselves as in showing Hawthorne's underlying concern with language. They are probably the most unintellectual form of verbal humor, depending only upon an elementary intellectual realization that one word may have more than one meaning. Certainly Hawthorne's word-plays are no gems of subtlety even within the rather broad and obvious limits imposed by the form. Yet his interest in them is important in any understanding of his comic style, for it is the interest of a stylist. Hawthorne is a master of subtlety of tone in language, and one might say that his use of the pun is the least subtle of the stylistic devices by which he achieves control over his linguistic medium.

Hawthorne's interest in language can be seen very clearly as well in his many notebook entries where he shows himself fascinated by words as abstract counters, divorced from any context other than their own. The famous notation, "To personify If—But—And—Though—&c"[12] is usually quoted by critics to show Hawthorne's preciousness, his divorce from reality, his lack of beef-and-ale. This may be true, but again it is not the whole story. It shows a fascination with the mechanics of language on the part of a man who habitually saw everything—persons, places, language, and ideas—as types or tropes of some supersensual reality. The same habit of mind occurs over and over again in the notebooks.

Hawthorne's observations often take the turn of the humorist who quietly analyses some ridiculous thing in terms of the most profound high seriousness. A kind of "shaggy dog" story in miniature exists in Hawthorne's apparently completely incredulous and naïve observation of a man he observed at Bridge's home in Maine, who was run away with by a literally horseless carriage. "Ludicrous situation of a man drawing his chaise down a sloping bank, to wash it in the river. The chaise got the better of him, and rushing downward, as if it were possessed, compelled him to run at full speed, and drove him up to his chin into the river. A singular instance, that a chaise may run away with a man, without a horse."[13] In addition to the ridiculousness of the situation, which gives the story most of its amusing effect, it is perhaps worth pointing out that the entry revolves around two rather obvious quibbles. The conception depends upon there being no horse before the cart, and is a sort of humorous comment upon Emerson's sober dictum that things are in the saddle and riding mankind—though here, of course, they are chaising him.

The best example of this type of folk humor is found in *Blithedale* through the observation, oddly enough, of Miles Coverdale, the poet-author. He tells, with a perfectly straight face, the scandalous charges which the farmers allege against the incompetence of the Blithedale colony.

> They had the face to say . . . that the cows laughed at our awkwardness at milking-time, and invariably kicked over the pails; partly in consequence of our putting the stool on the wrong side, and partly because, taking offence at the whisking of their tails, we were in the habit of holding these natural fly-flappers with one hand and milking with the other. They further averred that we hoed up whole acres of Indian corn and other crops, and drew the earth carefully about the weeds; and that we raised five hundred tufts of burdock, mistaking them for cabbages; and that, by dint of unskilful planting few of our seeds ever came up at all, or, if they did come up it was stern-foremost; and that we spent the better part of the month of June in reversing a field of beans, which had thrust themselves out of the ground in this unseemly way.[14]

The complexity of this joke is worth a brief note. As a generic type, of course, the charges against the transcendental brethren are part of the common pattern of the joke on the dude who doesn't know how to do the simplest of tasks, and it is quite fitting that they be brought against the Blithedale colony by society at large, to which Blithedale stands, as Coverdale has discovered, in a position of new hostility rather than new friendship.

The purpose of the joke is to cast ridicule on the Blithedale farmers, and the ridicule is of the broadest type. If the charges are true the colony stands condemned, but the fact of the matter is that the charges are not true, at least as they stand, and are not expected to be regarded as true. Indeed, to interpret them as either true or false is to miss the point of the joke, which serves a serious purpose while it makes us smile. First of all, the joke is true in its falsehood, to deal in paradox. If these charges were in fact true, these Blithedale farmers would be the kind of people to whom they would happen. The Blithedale community, by the very fact that these ridiculous charges can be brought against it and be believed, although everyone knows that they are not literally true, is made the object of the greatest contempt. The fact that these rumors can be circulated at all serves as a very accurate index of the lack of respect which society at large feels for the Blithedale experiment; and, as the story develops, society's opinion is shown to be true in essence, albeit false in expression, directly analogous to society's jokes about Blithedale. Secondly, these charges are the kind which in their very nature cannot be answered, even if Coverdale knows they are false. Their importance is psychological, rather than logical, and the victims of such a joke cannot deny the psychological validity of the charges by disproving their factual basis. The charges as such are not important; they are important only in that they give us an unsympathetic view of the Blithedale colony, a view which, much more than Coverdale's eventual intellectual disillusion, highlights the essential falsity of the Blithedale experiment. The artistic reason for the introduction of this type of joke is to show the stupidity of the attempt, and to give a hint at the colony's ultimate failure which, society says, is inherent in the people it attracts. This is the way Blithedale really is, not the way the colonists see it, and not only the way any of the principle characters see it.

The use of the ludicrous to drive home the point that the reality of a situation is something other than any perception of it by a character is one of Hawthorne's favorite devices. A startling example of it may be found in "Egotism." When Herkimer first meets Elliston, weaving down the street with a snake in his bosom, he is shocked. The situation is beyond the worst he has anticipated. As Elliston comes by, Herkimer accosts him.

> "Elliston! Roderick!" cried he, "I had heard of this; but my conception came far short of the truth. What has befallen you? Why do I find you thus?"
>
> "Oh, 't is a mere nothing! A snake! A snake! The commonest thing in the world. A snake in the bosom—that's all," answered Roderick Elliston.[15]

This passage cannot be read seriously; anyone who thinks it is solemn need only read it aloud to have his doubts instantly dispelled. The passage is an obvious take-off on the stilted dialogue of the melodrama, the "I have you now, my dark beauty!" type of thing later so common in the cheap thrillers. But why would Hawthorne ruin a dramatic moment such as this for the sake of a rather paltry joke? The answer I think lies in the fact that the symbol of the snake in the bosom is so ludicrous in itself that it would be fatal to treat it seriously.

The story operates on at least two levels. If we take it absolutely solemnly and seriously, the tragedy of Roderick Elliston is a great human catastrophe, and Hawthorne himself, in his note to the tale, vouches for the veracity of the phenomenon. Possession of a human being by supernatural agents and by devils has been a constantly obsessive thematic archetype of the western mind, preserved in folklore, and the basis of countless tales of undoubted mythic power. Nevertheless, no reader can possibly read "Egotism" this solemnly. The very fact that a man thinks he has a snake in his bosom, if proposed seriously, is occasion for a wry smile rather than a shock of horror on the part of the listener. On the other hand, the fact that a man could force himself to believe that he actually did have a snake in his bosom is certainly emblematic of the highest form of egotism, and that the whole thing is ridiculous on the face of it makes his belief all the more compelling. In addition, Elliston's reply is the Byronic reply at its lowest common denominator, when sardonic laughter has declined into smiling through. For this is the answer of the man who must laugh (desperately) to keep from weeping—but at what? At something we cannot really take seriously, at a snake in his bosom. By the use of the comic in this story Hawthorne has succeeded in very nicely avoiding the pitfall of pomposity to which all such tales are inherently subject, to make a commonplace point in an unconventional manner.

Everyone is willing to admit, at least for the sake of discussion, that we should not be egoistic, and probably will even confess when pressed that egotism has adverse effects upon the character. Yet how trivial an effect is the obsession with a snake in one's bosom, how utterly lacking in any kind of human value. And yet, Hawthorne suggests, this is the way egotism is—it does not make man into a tragic figure, but into a contemptible and slightly foolish one. This is a serious point, but it is one which can be made artistically only through comic means.

A somewhat less profound, but equally serious, use of humor is found in the story of Perseus in A Wonder-Book. Perseus, who has been sent off to kill a Gorgon, does so and brings her head back to King Polydectes, who has sent him on the quest. The Gorgon's head, it will be remembered, is death to look at, having the power to turn the beholder at once into stone, and Perseus has succeeded in killing the Gorgon only by viewing the head as reflected in his highly polished shield. When Perseus brings the head back to Polydectes, however, the King mentions that it, with its snaky locks, must be a "very curious spectacle." Suddenly Perseus gets his idea for revenge. He tells Polydectes: "Your Majesty is in the right . . . It is really an object that will be pretty certain to fix the regards of all who look at it. And, if your Majesty think fit, I would suggest that a holiday be proclaimed, and that all your Majesty's subjects be summoned to behold this wonderful curiosity. Few of them, I imagine, have seen a Gorgon's head before, and perhaps never may again!"[16]

The punning is again important. The head will "fix the re-gards" of the beholders, few of whom have ever seen one before or will ever see one again. At the same time, the situation is a wonderful satire on the enthusiastic hard sell of the door-to-door canvasser. The whole impression which Perseus gives is that this is a once-in-a-lifetime opportunity which will never again be offered, and he is quite right, although the effects of viewing the Gorgon's head are not precisely those which induce Polydectes to undertake the experience. The joke is clear enough, but why Hawthorne used it is another matter. In this situation one could apparently make the point seriously, or at least with-out resort to this gratuitous low comedy. But to say this is again to miss the implication of the comic mode. One *could* make the point seriously, but one *doesn't have to*. The whole value of humor in this tale lies in the implicit idea that the adven-ture *can* be comically viewed. The turning of Polydectes and all his courtiers to stone, though apparently sadistic and cruel, can be seen as a comic event. Hawthorne, by showing that a comic approach is possible, has succeeded in making the reality of the situation at once more ambiguous and more profound. At the same time, the unveiling of the Gorgon's head, the confrontation of Polydectes with a disastrous and completely unexpected reality, can be viewed in another, less serious way. The revenge tradition—for Polydectes had sent Perseus to kill the Gorgon expecting that Perseus himself would be killed—is, in this tale, viewed comically as well as tragically.

Hawthorne was committed to the point of view that comedy was not only of possible value in making a serious point, but that the omission of the comic was a grave error in any profound apprehension of reality. The serious and the solemn were not for him the same. To Horatio Bridge, who was sailing with the Navy up and down the African coast, doing battle with hostile natives and bearing up remarkably well under the white man's burden, Hawthorne wrote a very fine serio-comic letter. Bridge had written him, telling him of a brief skirmish which his party had had with some African tribesmen, and Hawthorne wrote back, advising Bridge to be more careful in the future.

> As your station, I believe, does not call you to the front of the battle, do pray be advised to stay on board ship the next time, and think how much preferable is a sluggish life to such a *slug*-gish death as you might chance to meet on shore. A civilized and educated man must feel somewhat like a fool, methinks, when he has staked his own life against that of a black savage and lost the game. In the sight of God one life may be as valuable as another, but in our view the stakes are very unequal. Besides, I really do consider the shooting of these negroes a matter of very questionable propriety, and am glad, upon the whole, that you bagged no game upon either of those days.[17]

How much better this is than a long and solemn tirade in which the evils of imperialism would be trotted out and counted over. The statement that "a civilized and educated man must feel somewhat like a fool . . . when he has staked his own life against that of a black savage and lost the game" is one of the finest touches ever written against the shabbiness of imperialism and the general hollowness of any such military glory. Bridge had been quite exuberant about this petty battle, which seemed to him to smack of high adventure. Hawthorne's opinions are quite otherwise. Though he speaks humorously, he can also speak frankly to an old friend, and he leaves no doubt that he finds the situation quite unheroic.

That comedy was central to Hawthorne's art was recognized by several of his contemporary critics, though most of them were uncertain whether it was a basic principle of his artistic vision or just a happy accident. One exception to this was Herman Melville, in his famous review of Hawthorne's *Mosses*, written before the two had ever met. Melville begins his praise of Hawthorne's humor rather conventionally. Specifically of the Old Manse he asks rhetorically: "What a wild moonlight of contemplative humor bathes that Old Manse! the rich and rare distilment of a spicy and slowly-oozing heart. No rollicking rudeness, no gross fun fed on fat dinners, and bred in the lees of wine,—but a humor so spiritually gentle, so high, and yet so richly relishable, that it were hardly inappropriate in an angel. It is the very religion of mirth; for nothing so human but it may be advanced to that." Yet he continues his probing of the comic spirit in a more serious vein, ultimately deciding that comedy for Hawthorne is neither an end in itself nor an accidental quality of his art. Rather, he says, it is an integral part of Hawthorne's vision, a mode of perception, an organizing principle through which he views the world. He concludes that such a high humor must postulate a deep understanding.

> There is no man, in whom humor and love, like mountain peaks, soar to such a rapt height as to receive the irradiations of the upper skies;—there is no man in whom humor and love are developed in that high form called genius; no such man can exist without also possessing, as the indispensable complement of these, a great, deep intellect, which drops down into the universe like a plummet. Or, love and humor are only the eyes through which such an intellect views this world.[18]

This "great, deep intellect" is what Hawthorne uses to discover that blackness in the universe which Melville found so striking. Melville sees here that for Hawthorne comedy and tragedy are complementary, and that high comedy and profound tragedy cannot exist apart from one another. That this is true in Melville's own case does not, I think, need emphasis, and because it is so obviously true of him its profundity when applied to Hawthorne has been overlooked and underemphasized. Melville's essay has been taken generally as of great significance in its explanations of Melville's own aesthetic, but without too much actual reference to Hawthorne. Actually, Melville has very accurately seen the basic significance of the comic in Hawthorne's artistic method, and his perceptions have all the more value since he arrived at them through a reading of the *Mosses,* and *not* by talking with Hawthorne himself. Consequently, his impressions have value as independent statements, and not merely as quasi-official explanations.

Insofar as Hawthorne is on record theoretically with regard to his use of comedy, he confirms Melville's point of view. For he feels that comedy and tragedy are inextricably mixed and can be separated only logically. One of the most famous passages in the Notebooks is relevant here; this is the origin of the idea later developed in "Earth's Holocaust": "When the reformation of the world is complete, a fire shall be made of the gallows; and the Hangman shall come and sit down by it, in solitude and despair. To him shall come the Last Thief, the Last Prostitute, the Last Drunkard, and other representatives of past crime and vice; and they shall hold a dismal merry-making, quaffing the contents of the Drunkard's last Brandy Bottle."[19] The interrelation of mirth and sadness is here stated concisely and, at least intellectually, completely. The phrase "dismal merry-making" is an arresting one. How many of Hawthorne's tales deal directly with this idea of dismal mirth! "The Christmas Banquet," "Dr. Heidegger's Experiment," "Young Goodman Brown," "The Wedding Knell," *The Blithedale Romance*, to mention only a few obvious examples. The house of feasting and the house of mourning are complementary, and a visit to one may often bring one unaware to the other.

"A virtuous but giddy girl to attempt to play a trick on a man. He sees what she is about, and contrives matters so that she throws herself completely into his power, and is ruined,—all in jest,"[20] Hawthorne wrote in his notebook in 1837, another clear statement of the interdependence of comedy and tragedy, or at least of the power of comedy to produce a serious effect. Another example of many may be given which says almost exactly the same thing: "The world is so sad and solemn, that things meant in jest are liable, by an overpowering influence, to become dreadful earnest,—gayly dressed fantasies turning to ghostly and black-clad images of themselves."[21]

A beautiful example of a "thing meant in jest" turning in spite of itself into something "dreadful earnest" may be found in the implied comparison in "Ethan Brand" of Ethan himself to the dog who unsuccessfully chases his tail in a sort of metaphorical statement of the central ethical dilemma in the story. Certainly "Ethan Brand" is one of Hawthorne's more stark and horrible tales, and certainly the comic elements in the story are very much subdued. Nevertheless, a dog chasing his tail is, when one stops to think of it, a very peculiar image with which to indicate the plight of a man in search of the Unpardonable Sin.[22] The basis for this story may be found in the Notebook entries Hawthorne kept at North Adams. North Adams apparently abounded with eccentric dogs which Hawthorne observed with fascination. The North Adams journal is a tissue of observations on canine behavior, not all of which by any means found their way into the story "Ethan Brand." Hawthorne's mind, though, was working with the intellectual conception behind "Ethan Brand," playing with the idea of the Unpardonable Sin, the "separation of the intellect from the heart,"[23] even when not applying it specifically to the story itself. The dog chasing his tail may well be an enigmatic symbol in itself, but some light is thrown on it by this further passage in the North Adams journal, a gloss which has hitherto passed unnoticed: "All dogs, of whatever different sizes and dissimilar varieties, acknowledge the common bond of species among themselves; and the largest one does not disdain to suffer his tail to be smelt of, nor to reciprocate that courtesy, to the smallest."[24] The point, of course, is not that this entry is a source for "Ethan Brand," which it rather obviously is not. It does show, however, that Hawthorne's mind could see in two quite different phenomena an exemplification of the same underlying idea. Moreover, the journal entry is very definitely humorous, as is, basically, the image of the dog's chasing his tail which forms the ironic counterpoint to Ethan Brand's quest for the Unpardonable Sin. An underlying thematic preoccupation is here seen in two ways which are quite different in kind, a conventionally humorous way and a tragically somber way.

Perhaps these remarks may serve as preamble to a discussion of the comic vision in *Blithedale*, a novel which R. R. Male, Jr., has brilliantly characterized as "the pastoral wasteland." *Blithedale* is conventionally regarded as a novel which explores the failure of comedy, a failure which is connected symbolically with the failure of the Blithedale colony. Blithedale is, one might say, a much more highly developed Merry Mount, where evil is denied by the fatuous method of ignoring it. Male has summed up this point of view very well when he says that "the failure of Blithedale may be summed up as a misplaced faith in the comic vision of life as a mode of emotional conversion. The essence of the comic vision, as Hawthorne considered it, lay in the breaking of bonds—links with the past, ties with social classes. As Melville's mentor Solomon said, there is 'a time to embrace, and a time to refrain from embracing,' and the communitarians have confused the tragic usefulness of the one with the comic purpose of the other."[25]

If we leave aside the rather doubtful assertion that the essence of the comic vision for Hawthorne lies in the breaking of bonds, the specific application to Blithedale is undoubtedly true. Yet it carries, as do most discussions of Hawthorne's comedy, the apparent implication that comedy is somehow less serious than tragedy. It would be better of course, if there were no necessity for choice, and anyone would admit that a society where embracing is neither useful nor purposeful would certainly be more placid and perhaps more desirable than the present imperfect state of things. But Solomon also reminds us that there is a time to live and a time to die, and that each depends upon the other. One cannot live, like Septimius Felton, by denying life, and the nightmare of life in death is a very real one for Hawthorne. The grave may be a fine and quiet place, but it is not the place for embracing, though it does not follow from this that embracing *in itself* is futile. The failure of the Blithedale experiment is rather that the colonists have made the unjustified assumption that embracing excludes not embracing, that the time to die will never come.

The great danger inherent in any interpretation of *Blithedale* as a comic novel in which in some sense the comedy is shown up as false comes in the critical statement of the idea that Miles Coverdale is in some way an anti-hero, or, at best, an impotent failure. This is, on the face of it, partially true. But it does not follow that Coverdale's failure is in any way his own fault, or subject to moral censure. Every interpretation of which I am aware of *The Blithedale Romance* either tacitly or explicitly accepts the idea that if Coverdale were somehow different, nobler, closer to an ideal, he would be a success and not a failure. Moreover, Coverdale *should* be better than he is, and because he is not Hawthorne must necessarily be satirizing him. This does not seem to me a just inference. If we were all perfect, certainly we would be better people, but the fact is that we are not all perfect, and the speculation becomes somewhat futile. Coverdale, it seems to me, is in a peculiar predicament in *Blithedale* because he is the only "two-eyed" man among a series of "one-eyed" types.[26] In a sense, in Hawthorne's terms, this reduces him to impotence, but his impotence is a special brand. It is not the quiescence of an inactive man as much as the realization of an intelligent one that all the ends he is asked to follow are more or less undesirable. Coverdale tries to make a success out of the Blithedale experiment because he believes in its truth. He resists Hollingworth's attempts to sabotage the experiment on grounds which are not grounds of impotence at all, but rather grounds of moral choice.

Coverdale's refusal to betray the colony and follow Hollingsworth is generally given grudging admiration which is immediately qualified by the reflection that his reaction is after all only negative. This assumes not only that a positive reaction is possible, a rather dangerous assumption, but that it is desirable as well. Coverdale's arguments in the Chapter "A Crisis," when Hollingsworth proposes his scheme, are not basically the statements of a position of impotence or of negativism. They are rather the affirmation of moral right against opportunism. Coverdale refuses to do a little wrong in order to accomplish even the greatest right, and Hollingsworth's philanthropic schemes have not even the value of common sense. Hollingsworth can prate all he wishes about Coverdale's life lacking "strength, courage, immitigable will," and containing only "aimless beauty," but this does not fool Coverdale into thinking for one moment that Hollingsworth's scheme is anything more than a gigantic swindle to sabotage the good faith of the community. Besides, we have only Hollingsworth's word that "aimless beauty" is silly. Hollingsworth, like Danforth in "The Artist of the Beautiful," is a blacksmith by trade, and his advice to Coverdale is rather remarkably like Danforth's advice to Owen Warland.

It would be better in this situation—abstractly considered—if Coverdale had a positive choice, but the fact is that he does not, and in this case a negative choice is better than a passive acquiescence. In situations such as this a man's only choice is a negative one, and to say Yes, as Melville saw so clearly, is to lie. Miles Coverdale, like Hawthorne, has the courage to say No.

Coverdale's negative choice, combined with his famous statement that he has no cause to believe in, but that he would be glad if one were to turn up, has led to the general critical conclusion that Coverdale's cynicism is a mark of weakness. The usual documentation of this is Coverdale's famous statement that, "If Kossuth, for example, would pitch the battlefield of Hungarian rights within an easy ride of my abode, and choose a mild, sunny morning, after breakfast, for the conflict, Miles Coverdale would gladly be his man, for one brave rush upon the levelled bayonets. Further than that, I should be loath to pledge myself."[27] It is easy to read this as a statement of denial of responsibility, or a refusal to fight at all for anything. Kossuth, the argument runs, is so far away as to be meaningless, and Coverdale's comments amount to a well-bred shrug of the shoulders. But this ignores the point that Coverdale has made earlier to Hollingsworth in denying his right to sabotage the Blithedale colony for his own ends. Hollingsworth has asked if he really believes that any of the Blithedale ideal will ever be transmuted into reality. Coverdale for once is serious in his reply. Reality will come, he says, as it always does, but "it will wear the every-day, commonplace, dusty, and rather homely garb, that reality always does put on."[28] And of course Reality does come to Blithedale, in the common guise of Zenobia's suicide. There is no need to search for trouble, Coverdale says, for it will find you of its own accord. Were Kossuth in America, Coverdale would fight for him. As it is, both of them must fight their own battles.

None of the autobiographical studies of *Blithedale* has noticed one interesting parallel between Miles Coverdale and Hawthorne which gives some credence to the idea that Coverdale might just possibly have been speaking seriously. When Hawthorne was told by Fields that the Dedication of *Our Old Home* to Franklin Pierce would be unwise and unpolitic he, like Miles

Coverdale, refused to compromise with principle. He wrote Fields that to retract the Dedication would be morally impossible for him, however it might be justified on grounds of expediency.

> I find that it would be piece of poltroonery in me to with-draw either the dedication or the dedicatory letter. My long and intimate relations with Pierce render the dedica-tion altogether proper, especially as regards this book, which would have had no existence without his kindness; and if he is so exceedingly unpopular that his name is enough to sink the volume, there is so much the more need that an old friend should stand by him. I cannot, merely on account of pecuniary profit or literary reputation, go back from what I have deliberately thought and felt it right to do; and if I were to tear out the dedication, I should never look at the volume again without remorse and shame.[29]

Accordingly, the book was dedicated to Pierce and the storm of criticism with which the Dedication was received amply jusified Fields's apprehensions. But Hawthorne had been true to his principles, unpopular as they might be; he had not sought trouble, yet when it came, like Miles Coverdale he was good for one rush upon the bayonets.

Hawthorne's view of the comic, then, was that it was a neces-sary part of any realistic apprehension of Reality. The failure of the comic in *Blithedale* is not Coverdale's failure, but rather the failure of the Blithedale colonists and of Hollingsworth to make allowance for the tragic. This is exactly the failure of the Merry Mount colony, and one might extend this index of failure to all of Hawthorne's miscellaneous crowd of reformers who refuse to look at Reality as in any way tragic. Although to the best of my knowledge there is no character in Hawthorne's fiction whose failure can be laid solely to his denial of the comic principle, to his perception of the tragic alone unrelieved by the comic, nevertheless Hawthorne does deal with a related conception, the idea of the oneness of pleasure and pain or, by a not wholly unjustified extension, of tragedy and comedy. George Parsons Lathrop has briefly mentioned the "possible identity of love and hate"[30] in the relationship between Coverdale and Hollingsworth in *Blithedale;* but more to the point is Hawthorne's own analysis of this identity in the character of Chillingworth in *The Scarlet Letter.*

> It is a curious subject of observation and inquiry, whether hatred and love be not the same thing at bottom. Each, in its utmost development, supposes a high degree of intimacy and heart-knowledge; each renders one individual dependent for the food of his affections and spiritual life upon another; each leaves the passionate lover, or the no less passionate hater, forlorn and desolate by the withdrawal of his subject. Philosophically considered, therefore, the two passions seem essentially the same, except that one happens to be seen in a celestial radiance, and the other in a dusky and lurid glow. In the spiritual world, the old physician and the minister—mutual victims as they have been—may, unawares, have found their earthly stock of hatred and antipathy transmuted into golden love.[31]

For purpose of this discussion the significance of this remark lies not so much in the psychological acuteness of this observation as in the more metaphysical statement of the unity behind two apparently diverse forces. Hawthorne gives here a dichotomy of effects which depends upon a uniform underlying cause. Chillingworth's attitude toward Dimmesdale might be expressible in two terms which are apparent opposites—love and hatred. Nevertheless, each of these attitudes depends upon the action of one peculiar cause—in this case, the relationship of Chillingworth to the man who has wronged him. In other words, a given cause—Dimmesdale's "wronging" of Chillingworth—can give rise to two distinct and opposite impressions, or, put in another way, can be understood by means of two opposite attitudes. The Reality itself, the fact which Chillingworth observes, can be analyzed in terms of either "love" or "hatred" or of both together. The two passions which Hawthorne says seem to be the same in essence are different only in the mode by which they perceive Reality. Chillingworth has perceived Reality only through hatred;

a more noble man might perceive it through love; and a wiser man could perceive it through both together. Chillingworth's failure, then, although not a failure of the tragic vision, is in fact analogous to it. His failure is the failure of the one-eyed man maddened by the tragic vision and unrelieved by the comic spirit. Chillingworth has been diabolized by his too tragic perception of evil, unregenerated by the sanative effect of comedy.

Indeed, the larger serious purpose of comedy in Hawthorne's vision seems to be that it has a sanative effect. It offers a method for perceiving the meaning of experience which enables one to understand rationally, to give one some control over the unchecked tragic play of the emotions. The comic spirit depends upon the tragic vision because humor is impossible if the joke is not taken seriously, yet the comic spirit itself is a means of handling experience which is neither morbid nor unrealistic. The comic vision is a sign of the healthy mind, not only, as might first appear, because an untroubled man can laugh, but because he has learned to see himself from two points of view, to cut his tragic pretensions down to a more realistic external human measure.

Hawthorne makes this point most clearly in his discussion of two characters. The first, Clifford, in *Seven Gables,* is the most broken and helpless of all Hawthorne's major fictional people. He has seen the terror at the heart of existence and it has broken him, rendering him unable to laugh. When an organ-grinder comes underneath his window he sees in the ugly monkey a symbolic statement of his own pathetic plight, and his reaction is characteristic.

> He had taken childish delight in the music, and smiled, too, at the figure which it set in motion. But, after looking a while at the long-tailed imp, he was so shocked by his horrible ugliness, spiritual as well as physical, that he actually began to shed tears; a weakness which men of merely delicate endowments, and destitute of the fiercer, deeper, and more tragic power of laughter, can hardly avoid, when the worst and meanest aspect of life happens to be presented to them.[32]

It takes a strong-minded man to laugh precisely for the reason that Clifford weeps. There *is* a good analogy between the monkey and Clifford, between the monkey and everyman, between the ridiculous and the human. And the analogy is what the weak-minded will not choose to see.

The second, Kenyon, in *The Marble Faun,* is a different sort of person. He is one of the comparatively few characters in Hawthorne's fiction with both a tragic and a comic view of Reality. Like Miles Coverdale he is an artist, though perhaps a better one, and like Coverdale he has a gift of laughter which depends upon a perception of the infinite sadness of things. When, toward the end of *The Marble Faun,* he brings about the eventual resolution of the action, the result is pathetic in the extreme. He realizes that the reunion which he has effected between Miriam and Donatello must in its very nature be temporary, that it must be dissolved by the very moral choice which brought it about, for Miriam and Donatello must give themselves up to what is both ironically and in dead seriousness "justice." Love, in the case of these two at once pitiable and admirable lovers, has caused its own dissolution; the one principle in the world which works for stability has reduced itself to chaos. At the same time, Hilda is gone and Kenyon knows not where, though Miriam and Donatello have assured him that she will be returned to him at the Carnival. Tortured by sadness which is not only personal, Kenyon plunges into the Roman Carnival, the epitome of commercialized mirth, to his promised rendezvous with Hilda. Kenyon is sad enough to feel completely foreign to the Carnival spirit, and Hawthorne suggests that this is a natural enough human feeling. Yet it is an erroneous one, though understandable. A wiser man would have taken the Carnival as it came, and not have set himself in opposition to it.

> Kenyon, though young, had care enough within his breast to render the Carnival the emptiest of mockeries. Contrasting the stern anxiety of his present mood with the frolic spirit of the preceding year, he fancied that so much trouble had, at all events, brought wisdom in its train. But there is a wisdom that looks grave, and sneers at merriment; and again a deeper wisdom, that stoops to be gay as often as occasion

serves, and oftenest avails itself of shallow and trifling grounds of mirth; because, if we wait for more substantial ones, we seldom can be gay at all . . . Kenyon would have done well to mask himself in some wild, hairy visage, and plunge into the throng of other maskers, as at the Carnival before.[33]

What Kenyon has done is to make the common yet erroneous equation between seriousness and sobriety, assuming that a sober look means a serious mind. To point up this falsity in his understanding, Hilda is released to him at the height of the shabby and commercialized Carnival mirth.

Yet though Hilda and Kenyon are in the Carnival they are really not of it, albeit related to it in a curious sense. The Carnival mirth is in itself silly and cheap, yet it expresses a deeper Reality, the reality of the comic vision, which Kenyon and Hilda cannot afford to ignore. Indeed, their two friends, who know much more of tragedy than Kenyon and Hilda, have not disdained to play the game of comedy as a final gesture before surrendering themselves to their tragic destiny. When Kenyon meets Miriam and Donatello in all the frenzied mirth of the Roman festival he meets a living emblem of Hawthorne's comic spirit, two masked revelers rejoicing in the tragic power of laughter.

Conclusion

I T IS JUST as well to admit frankly that in any discussion such as the foregoing the language of criticism must be distorted and oversimplified. In my analysis of Hawthorne's various techniques I have found it necessary to treat each one as if it existed more or less by itself. I have spoken of Hawthorne's humor, of his symbols, of his plots, of his ideas, as if each of these qualities existed apart from the others. Every student of Hawthorne knows how false this is. Hawthorne's symbols have a strange way of taking on a life of their own; his humor turns into tragedy, and both into pathos; his most abstract images have a way of acquiring a variety of ideological and intellectual connotations, oftentimes exact opposites. All the elements of Hawthorne's tales are mutually interdependent, and to discuss one in all its implications would inevitably require a discussion of every other element in the tale itself in relation to all the other things which Hawthorne wrote. Wherever one chooses to begin, he is led ever deeper into the tangled skein of apparently contradictory meanings, of seemingly diverse orders of reality, of purposely ambiguous symbols and concepts. Yet this in itself is, I think, the best illustration of my thesis. For to discuss Hawthorne at all, the critic must simplify him to a point where he becomes unrecognizable. Any attempt to bring a simple order out of his apparently diffuse and chaotic world is foredoomed to failure; Hawthorne's world is not amenable to order. The order which the critic attempts to impose upon Hawthorne's artistic vision is of a type with the order which Hawthorne's characters attempt to apply to their various fictional worlds. Both types of order are possible only by ignoring certain aspects of experience; and each, through its failure, indirectly affirms Hawthorne's central artistic contention—the multiplicity inherent in apparent unity.

Without being in the slightest bit facetious one could well conclude this study by calling it inconclusive. For, if anything, this is the only result at which one can arrive in a study of Hawthorne. I have suggested that Hawthorne, as a Platonist in a very peculiar sense, has an intellectual commitment to the idea of two worlds, the Real world of Being and the Apparent world of Becoming, both of which are related, but only one of which is knowable. The two worlds are related by analogies—our perception of effects in the world of Becoming posits, for Hawthorne at least, the undoubted existence of the world of Being. Nevertheless, this world of Being cannot be truly known in any other way than by recognizing the validity of the analogy. Hawthorne discusses the relation of the two worlds most clearly and most carefully in his stories dealing with the problem of artistic creation, with the problem of how the artist creates his work of art. In these discussions of the nature of artistic creation Hawthorne emphasizes particularly two related themes. First is the idea that the artist creates his work of art from some Ideal form which only he can see and understand; second is the idea that the work of art as it is created is in its nature an imperfect copy of the Ideal form. Notably in "The Artist of the Beautiful" and in Kenyon's discussion of his work in *The Marble Faun* the idea is emphatically stated that art-works are imperfect copies of ideal forms, and that perfect beauty, which the artist attempts to copy, can be found only in the world of Being, the world of super-experiential Reality. Nevertheless, by the very fact that this art-work exists and because Hawthorne postulates a relationship between it and its Ideal prototype, however imperfect a copy the work of art may be, the existence and importance of the Real world, as opposed to the Apparent, is constantly affirmed. The Real world is that which gives the Apparent its form, that upon which the existence of the Apparent world is dependent.

The important point about this analogy between the two worlds, however, is that the relationship between them can be stated *only* in terms of the analogy, and the knowledge of the existence of this analogical relationship, coupled with whatever factual knowledge we may possess of the world of Becoming, cannot give us any insight into the Reality of the world of

Being. Consequently, although Hawthorne always intellectually posits the relationship between the two worlds, and although he is constantly interested in the light which the knowledge of this relationship throws on the imperfections in the Apparent world, and although he seems personally to believe that the imperfections of the world of Becoming will be made perfect in the world of Being, still, his artistic concern is really not with the world of Being at all, but with the world of Becoming, the world of Appearances, the world of everyday. This interest in the world of Appearances is where Hawthorne is at his least conventionally Platonic, not so much in his thought as in his emphasis. For the traditional concern of Platonic thought has been with the Real world rather than the Apparent. Traditionally, Platonic philosophers have assumed, and Hawthorne follows them in their basic assumptions, that the Apparent world is a somewhat enigmatic symbol of the Real; from this, they have attempted to order perceived experience so that by it they might obtain a rational insight into the world of Being. Their failure, it need not be remarked, has been singularly notable. Inherent in such an approach lies mysticism, and the best of the Platonists have always been mystically inclined. But mysticism is in itself a confession of epistemological failure, a tacit admission that a knowledge of the analogical relation between the two worlds does not in itself bring any knowledge of the world of Being. Though Platonic, in a loose sense, in his admission of the difference between the Real world and the Apparent, Hawthorne is heretical in his interest in the Apparent in and for itself.

A cherished tenet of all Platonists has been that the Real world differs from the Apparent on the basis of its greater simplicity. The Apparent world is diffuse, complex, contradictory, incomplete; the Real world is simple, complete, and unified. Hawthorne accepts this Platonic notion as well, in order to explain the difference between the two worlds, but again his emphasis is unorthodox. Rather than attempting to reduce complexity to unity and by so doing to arrive at a knowledge of the guiding principle behind apparent opposites, he accepts these opposites, these apparent contradictions, and studies them in and for themselves. And, although the study of opposites and ap-

parent contradictions may give us a further insight into the world of Being, it is an *a fortiori* insight, a multiplication of the force of the analogy by multiplying the number of apparently diverse phenomena. In short, Hawthorne's philosophical proof of the analogical relationship itself seems to be that multiplicity posits Unity through the very force of its diversity. The very fact that there can be so many contradictory explanations for a thing, each one of which is tenable, proves only that all are incomplete and fragmentary, and reinforces the belief in some simple explanation which encompasses all the possible fragmentary ones. What this complete explanation is, however, Hawthorne does not say, and, indeed, implies that it is in its nature unknowable. All we can know is the *fact* that the Apparent is fragmentary and incomplete, and that the Real is not; what the Real is, we cannot, in the nature of things, know.

As a result, Hawthorne's literary endeavor becomes a constant search for more ways to emphasize the diversity of things. He attempts in his symbolic structure to show the presence of two or more different orders of Reality, and by his philosophical and ethical analyses to show the diversity of interpretation to which human action is liable. He attempts to show, through his insistence on the reader's duty to accept apparently incongruous symbols and events as in some sense Real, that at least one type of Reality is perhaps ludicrous and certainly not what we would expect it to be without investigation. His insistence upon our accepting the proper point of view in order to read his tales is another way of emphasizing this, of stating that the Reality of the tale is not objective but subjective, that it depends upon the reader himself and upon his willingness to hold in suspension two or more apparently contradictory points of view without asking for their reconciliation. And, by his use of humor to achieve serious ends and through his emphasis on the oneness of the Reality underlying comedy and tragedy, he emphasizes again the diversity of attitudes possible toward a given event or series of events. His constant efforts to elaborate his tales in terms of their symbolism and of the possible meanings inherent in them is a striking example of this attempt to include all the possible aspects of Reality in a given symbol, or attitude, or

train of events. This is best seen by comparing the various recently published preliminary sketches for the posthumous romances, which clearly show the constant process of elaboration
of detail which went on in Hawthorne's mind from first draft
to final form of a work of art. Subsidiary evidence of the same
type of revision can also be found by noticing the constant elaboration which some of his favorite themes undergo from the
time of the first Notebook entry to the date of the published
tale and sometimes between one earlier tale and a later one.

This constant elaboration of symbolic detail, coupled with
Hawthorne's favorite device of many explanations for the meaning of a given action, has been at once the despair and the
hope of his critics. This "ambiguity" has been seen variously as
a tough-minded facing up to experience, unwillingness to give
the pat answer, and conversely, as a defect in artistic vision, an
inability to make up one's mind, a lack of sharpness in the statement of artistic problems. Striking critical unawareness of the
possible function of this apparent ambiguity is evident in the
various interpretations given to Hawthorne's tales, readings
which invariably rest upon one or more quotations lifted from
a character who is assumed on no very good authority to be a
mouthpiece for Hawthorne's ideas.

The two best examples of this kind of reading may be found
in interpretations of *The Scarlet Letter* and *The Marble Faun.*
In the former, the argument rages around whether Dimmesdale's
remark that his and Hester's sin "had a consecration of its own"
is to be accepted at face value or not; in the latter, the question
of whether or not the tale is a defense or an attack upon the
concept of the Fortunate Fall depends upon whose arguments—
Hilda's, Kenyon's, or Miriam's—one accepts as true.

To my mind, all these statements, apparently contradictory as
they are, are contradictory for a very good purpose, to show the
various possible interpretations of a given action. None of these
interpretations has any ultimate or absolute metaphysical validity, but all are true in a limited way, in that they represent an
attempt to order experience and to give it meaning. The fact
that all these attempts to order experience are different is precisely Hawthorne's point, that all human interpretations of any-

thing whatever differ from each other, and that in any sense of reflecting the ultimate truth, the Truth of the world of Being, all are insufficient. But, paradoxically, each of these truths has relevance in the world of Becoming, both as showing the way in which a man—not Man in general—orders experience, and in casting light on the characters who offer these opinions. The fact that the opinions expressed by the characters are not necessarily those of the author at once relieves Hawthorne of the charge of didacticism and shows the subtlety with which he could envision alternative points of view toward a given phenomenon.

Hawthorne, in other words, accepts the Platonic position stated so well by Shelley near the end of *Adonaïs*:

> The One remains, the many change and pass;
> Heaven's light forever shines, Earth's shadows fly;
> Life, like a dome of many-coloured glass,
> Stains the white radiance of Eternity,
> Until Death tramples it to fragments.

But his emphasis is on the Many, not on the One, on the many colors of life rather than on the white radiance of Eternity, and his artistic endeavor is constantly to show as many colors as possible, and only very rarely to attempt to synthesize them into unity. Hawthorne himself once used a phrase for his philosophical beliefs, "Man's accidents are God's purposes," and it is more significant than might at first appear. The conventional Platonist, the philosopher in the grand tradition of Platonic thought, would have put it just the other way around: "God's purposes are Man's accidents." For him the accent would be on God and purpose; for Hawthorne it is on Man and accident.

Notes

CHAPTER I: *The Nature of Reality*

1. George Parsons Lathrop, "Introductory Note" to *Mosses from an Old Manse,* in *The Complete Works of Nathaniel Hawthorne with Introductory Notes by George Parsons Lathrop* (13 vols.; Boston and New York: Houghton, Mifflin and Company, 1882), II, 7-8. Subsequent references to Hawthorne's works, unless otherwise noted, will be to this edition, the Riverside Edition, hereafter referred to as *Works.* The inscription may still be seen in the Old Manse in Concord.

2. *The Light Beyond: A Study of Hawthorne's Theology* (Westminster, Maryland: The Newman Press, 1955), p. 173.

3. " 'Eternal Truth': A Study of Nathaniel Hawthorne's Philosophy," (Unpublished doctoral dissertation in the Indiana University Library), p. 48.

4. "Chiefly About War Matters," *Works,* XII, 331-32.

5. *Life of Franklin Pierce, Works,* XII, 417.

6. *Return to the Fountains: Some Classical Sources of American Criticism* (Durham, North Carolina: Duke University Press, 1942), pp. 68-78. Hawthorne also studied Plato in excerpts at Bowdoin. See Randall Stewart, *Nathaniel Hawthorne: A Biography* (New Haven: Yale University Press, 1948), pp. 16-17.

7. *The Puritan Mind* (New York: Henry Holt and Company, 1930), p. 135.

8. Among other books of a loosely Platonic cast, Hawthorne read Carlyle's *Essays;* various works of Coleridge; Shelley's Keats's, and Wordsworth's poems; Fuller's *Holy and Profane States;* works of Cotton, Increase, and Samuel Mather, and of Jeremy Taylor. See Marion L. Kesselring, *Hawthorne's Reading, 1828-1850. A Transcription and Identification of Titles Recorded in the Charge-Books of the Salem Athenaeum* (New York: The New York Public Library, 1949), pp. 43-64.

9. Letter to Delia Bacon, June 21, 1856. Quoted in Theodore Bacon, *Delia Bacon. A Biographical Sketch* (Boston and New York: Houghton, Mifflin and Company, 1888), p. 184.

10. *"The Marble Faun* Reconsidered," *UKCR,* XX (Spring, 1954), 193-99.

11. *American Renaissance: Art and Expression in the Age of Emerson and Whitman* (London: Oxford University Press, 1941), pp. 282-84.

Notes   163

12. *"The Scarlet Letter* and Its Modern Critics," *Nineteenth-Century Fiction,* VII (March, 1953), 251-54.

13. The best example of Hawthorne's denial of editorial responsibility may be seen in the various discussions of the meaning of the letter in the concluding chapter of *The Scarlet Letter.*

14. *Twice-Told Tales,* in *Works,* I, 218.

15. *Works,* I, 250.

16. "The Theme of Hawthorne's 'Fancy's Show Box'," *AL,* X (November, 1938), 341-43.

17. *Works,* I, 257.

18. *Mosses,* in *Works,* II, 235-36.

19. *Works,* II, 235, 251.

20. *Twice-Told Tales,* in *Works,* I, 128.

21. See below, pp. 42-45. The reader will recall the analysis (above, pp. 22-24) of the different points of view in "David Swan."

22. "'Eternal Truth'," p. 258. See also his "Hawthorne's 'Mrs. Bullfrog' and *The Rambler,*" *PQ,* XXXII (October, 1953), 382-87, for a study of Dr. Johnson's influence on the story.

23. See his Introduction to *The Portable Hawthorne* (New York: The Viking Press, 1948), pp. 9-10.

24. *Works,* II, 149. Cf. Hawthorne's remark in the American Notebooks for 1836: "Those who are very difficult in choosing wives seem as if they take none of Nature's ready-made works, but want a woman manufactured particularly to their order." *Passages from the American Note-Books,* in *Works,* IX, 32. According to Elizabeth Chandler's tabulations in *A Study of the Sources of the Tales and Romances Written by Nathaniel Hawthorne before 1853, Smith College Studies in Modern Language,* VII (July, 1926), "Mrs. Bullfrog" was written in the Autumn of 1835 or the Winter of 1835-36.

25. *Works,* II, 158.

26. E. L. Chandler, ed., "Hawthorne's 'Spectator'," *NEQ,* IV (April, 1931), 298.

27. *Works,* III, 377.

28. "'My Kinsman, Major Molineaux [*sic*]: An Interpretation," *UKCR,* XXI (March, 1955), 209.

29. Just what the ultimate meaning which Robin perceives in the symbolic degradation of Major Molyneux actually *is* is not germane to my discussion here. The subtlest interpretation of the tale of which I am aware is by Mrs. Q. D. Leavis, who sees it as a historical parable of America's coming of age told in terms of the ritual drama of "the conquest of the old king by the new." (*Sewanee Review,* LIX [Spring, 1951], 204.)

30. "A New Reading of *The Blithedale Romance,*" *AL,* XXIX (May, 1957), 147-70.

31. *Works,* III, 415.

32. *Works,* II, 361.
33. *Works,* III, 437.
34. *Works,* VI, 75-77.
35. *Works,* VI, 140-41.
36. *Mosses,* in *Works,* II, 258.
37. *Works,* VI, 430-31.
38. *Mosses,* in *Works,* II, 535-36.
39. *Mosses,* in *Works,* II, 529.
40. *The Snow-Image,* in *Works,* III, 508-9.
41. "A Select Party," *Mosses,* in *Works,* II, 83.
42. *Works,* II, 83.
43. "Hawthorne's 'Prophetic Pictures'," *AL,* XXIII (May, 1951), 188-202.
44. "Sights from a Steeple," *Twice-Told Tales, Works,* I, 220.
45. *Op. cit.,* p. 188.
46. *Op. cit.,* p. 192.
47. *Works,* I, 193.
48. *Works,* I, 202.
49. *Works,* I, 193.
50. *Works,* I, 203.
51. *Works,* I, 203.
52. *Works,* I, 207.
53. Randall Stewart, however, in Chapters III and IV of his Introduction to *The American Notebooks* (New Haven: Yale University Press, 1932), classifies Aylmer with the "Scholar-Idealists"—Fanshawe, the anonymous guest in "The Ambitious Guest," Owen Warland, Clifford Pyncheon in *The House of the Seven Gables,* and Dimmesdale in *The Scarlet Letter*—rather than with any of the three types of Hawthorne's villains. Mary A. Magginis, in her doctoral dissertation "Hawthorne's Comments on the Arts as Evidence of an Aesthetic Theory" in the University of North Carolina library, has suggested that "the common bond between all artists" is "the attempt to recreate beauty in various media," (p. 440) implying that these media are not necessarily confined to what one generally thinks of as "art." Frederick Crews, in his excellent study of *The Blithedale Romance,* has pointed out that "the Blithedale colony and Coverdale's Blithedale romance are both representative of the ideal," the one of moral and the other of aesthetic perfection, both demanding some sort of transcendence of the everyday world (*op. cit.,* 153). To these various representations of the Ideal, the scientific, as represented by Aylmer's quest for ideal feminine beauty, may legitimately be added.
54. "Rappaccini's Daughter," *Mosses,* in *Works,* II, 116.
55. *Works,* II, 61.
56. *The English Notebooks by Nathaniel Hawthorne* (New York: Modern Language Association of America, 1941), pp. 432-33

(November 20, 1856). Harrison Hayford, in "Hawthorne, Melville, and the Sea," *NEQ*, XIX (December, 1946), 435-52, has suggested that these conversations were not always so serious, but that Melville and Hawthorne spent a good deal of time "yarning" about the sea.

CHAPTER II: *The Nature of Artistic Illusion*

1. Preface to *The House of the Seven Gables*, in *Works*, III, 13. For a good discussion of Hawthorne's literary theory as developed in his Prefaces see Jesse Bier, "Hawthorne on the Romance: His Prefaces Related and Examined," *MP*, LIII (August, 1955), 17-24.

2. Preface to *Seven Gables*, *Works*, III, 13.

3. Quoted in James T. Fields, *Hawthorne* (Boston: James R. Osgood and Company, 1876), p. 29.

4. *Mosses*, in *Works*, II, 107.

5. *Mosses*, in *Works*, II, 107-8.

6. *Mosses*, in *Works*, II, 108.

7. March 19, 1850. Quoted in Harold Blodgett, "Hawthorne as Poetry Critic; Six Unpublished Letters to Lewis Mansfield," *AL*, XII (May, 1940), 182.

8. February 10, 1850. "Hawthorne as Poetry Critic," pp. 177-78.

9. *Works*, I, 16.

10. *Works*, I, 17.

11. *The Snow-Image*, *Works*, III, 439.

12. *Works*, III, 439-40. This latter catastrophe, a broken wire, does actually bring the show to a sudden stop just after the Great Snow of 1717.

13. *Works*, III, 442.

14. *Works*, III, 447-48.

15. *Works*, III, 454-55.

16. *Works*, III, 465, 476.

17. *Works*, I, 33-34.

18. See James T. Fields, *Hawthorne*, pp. 20-21; also Nelson F. Adkins, "The Early Projected Works of Nathaniel Hawthorne," *Papers of the Bibliographical Society of America*, XXXIX (April-June, 1945), 119-55.

19. *Symbolism and American Literature* (Chicago: University of Chicago Press, 1953), p. 10.

20. "The Custom House," in *Works*, V, 57.

21. Throughout this chapter I use the terms "Romance" and "Romantic" in opposition to "Novel" and "Novelistic" in the sense only of the type of fiction which Hawthorne wrote.

22. Preface to *The Marble Faun*, in *Works*, VI, 15.

23. "Hawthorne and the Twilight of Romance," *Yale Review*, XXXVII (March, 1948), 487-506.

24. *Works,* VI, 522-23.

25. *Letters of Hawthorne to William D. Ticknor, 1851-1864* (2 vols.; Newark, New Jersey: The Carteret Book Club, 1910), pp. 99-100.

26. *A Wonder Book, Works,* IV, 76.

27. *Works,* IV, 102.

28. *Works,* IV, 134.

29. *Works,* IV, 135.

30. *Works,* IV, 135-36.

31. Letter to Fields, May 23, 1851. Quoted in Fields, *Hawthorne,* pp. 32-33.

CHAPTER III: *Hawthorne's "Allegory"*

1. *Hawthorne's Fiction: The Light and the Dark* (Norman, Oklahoma: University of Oklahoma Press, 1952), p. 41.

2. "Hawthorne," in *American Prose Masters. Cooper—Hawthorne—Emerson—Poe—Lowell—Henry James* (New York: Charles Scribner's Sons, 1909), pp. 82, 80.

3. *Hawthorne's Fiction,* p. 7.

4. *Symbolism and American Literature,* p. 15.

5. "Hawthorne and the Twilight of Romance," *op. cit.,* p. 504.

6. Introduction to *The Complete Novels and Selected Tales of Nathaniel Hawthorne* (New York: The Modern Library, 1937), p. xiii.

7. *Hawthorne's Fiction,* pp. 13-14, 68-69.

8. *Hawthorne, A Critical Study* (Cambridge, Mass.: Harvard University Press, 1955), p. 58.

9. "A Masque of Love and Death," *University of Toronto Quarterly,* XXIII (October, 1953), 11.

10. Hawthorne does occasionally use the term in reference to his preliminary notes for stories. See, for example, *The American Notebooks,* ed. Randall Stewart, pp. 89, 90, 93.

11. See *Works,* II, 303.

12. *Works,* I, 527.

13. Hawthorne borrowed various volumes of the *Gentleman's Magazine,* the *Edinburgh Review, Blackwood's Magazine,* and other eighteenth-century periodicals from the Salem Athenaeum. He also withdrew *Antar, a Bedoueen Romance* on June 25, 1836. See M. L. Kesselring, *Hawthorne's Reading,* pp. 43-64.

14. See William Bysshe Stein, *Hawthorne's Faust: A Study of the Devil Archetype* (Gainesville, Florida: University of Florida Press, 1953), pp. 36-37.

15. *Works,* I, 528-30.

16. *Works,* I, 538. This story forms a positive exploration of a

theme which fascinated Hawthorne, man's finding his proper place in society. See above, pp. 26-27.

17. See John W. Shroeder, " 'That Inward Sphere': Notes on Hawthorne's Heart Imagery and Symbolism," *PMLA*, LXV (March, 1950), 106-19.

18. The story was put in the miscellaneous pieces in the Riverside Edition by George Parsons Lathrop.

19. *Works*, XII, 51.

20. *Works*, XII, 67.

21. Hawthorne assures us, for example, that the Reverend Mr. Hooper's wearing of a black veil in "The Minister's Black Veil" has a basis in fact. Similarly, "Wakefield," he says, springs from a story in a magazine or newspaper, and "The Prophetic Pictures," according to his note, has its factual basis in a story in Dunlap's *History of the Art of Design*.

22. Introduction to *The American Notebooks*, p. xlvii.

23. *Works*, II, 320.

24. *Works*, I, 325.

25. "The Moment and the Endless Voyage: A Study of Hawthorne's 'Wakefield'," *Diameter*, I (March, 1951), 7-12.

26. The first and third of these four tales are Kafka's "Metamorphosis" and "Ein Hungerkünstler."

27. *Works*, II, 430.

28. *Works*, II, 453.

29. *Works*, II, 447-48.

30. *Works*, II, 224.

31. *Works*, II, 196-97.

32. *Works*, II, 201.

33. *Works*, II, 201.

CHAPTER IV: *Plot as a Vehicle of Symbolic Meaning*

1. *Hawthorne's Last Phase* (New Haven: Yale University Press, 1949). Davidson's edition of the sketches for the various posthumous works has shown that, although all the romances were thematically closely allied, still each one was separately conceived.

2. Introductory Note to *The Ancestral Footstep*, *Works*, XI, 435-36.

3. *Nathaniel Hawthorne and His Wife: A Biography* (2 vols.; Boston and New York: Houghton, Mifflin and Company, 1884), I, 360.

4. Introductory Note to *The Scarlet Letter*, *Works*, V, 13.

5. *Hawthorne, the Artist: Fine-Art Devices in Fiction* (Chapel Hill: University of North Carolina Press, 1944). p. 176.

6. *Hawthorne, the Artist,* p. 138.

7. *American Renaissance,* p. 275.

8. "Form and Content in *The Scarlet Letter,*" *NEQ,* XVII (March, 1944), 25.

9. "One Hundred Years Ago: Hawthorne Set a Great New Pattern," *New York Herald Tribune Books* (August 6, 1950), pp. 1, 13.

10. *Hawthorne, the Artist,* p. 35.

11. "Hawthorne's House of Tradition," *South Atlantic Quarterly,* LII (October, 1953), 570.

12. "Hawthorne's House of Tradition," p. 569.

13. "Hawthorne's House of Tradition," p. 571.

14. "The Genius of Nathaniel Hawthorne," *North American Review,* CXXIX (September, 1879), 220.

15. *Hawthorne's Last Phase,* p. 31.

16. "Dr. Heidegger's Experiment," according to E. L. Chandler's calculations, was probably written in the Autumn of 1836. The earliest indication of Hawthorne's interest in the subject of immortality on earth is an 1836 entry in the *Notebooks*: "Curious to imagine what murmurings and discontent would be excited, if any of the great so-called calamities of human beings were to be abolished,—as, for instance, death." *Passages from the American Note-Books, Works,* IX, 36. An earlier entry for 1835 shows interest in a related theme. "Follow out the fantasy of a man taking his life by instalments, instead of at one payment,—say ten years of his life alternately with ten years of suspended animation." *Passages, Works,* IX, 27.

17. "Hawthorne's Methods of Using his Source Materials," in *Studies for William A. Read,* eds. Nathaniel M. Caffee and Thomas A. Kirby (Baton Rouge, Louisiana: Louisiana State University Press, 1940), pp. 301-12.

18. Pp. 305-6.

19. P. 307.

20. *The American Notebooks,* ed. Randall Stewart, p. 107.

21. *Works,* I, 487.

22. "On the Dog's Chasing His Own Tail in 'Ethan Brand'," *PMLA,* LXVIII (December, 1953), 975-81. For the Notebook entry—which is also quoted in the article—see *The American Notebooks,* ed. Randall Stewart, pp. xxxviii and 59.

23. An easily accessible example of Hawthorne's self-questioning may be found at the end of "Part II" of the published version of *The Ancestral Footstep,* in *Works,* XI, 491.

24. *The American Notebooks,* ed. Randall Stewart, pp. xxxiii-xxxiv, 90-92.

25. *The American Notebooks,* ed. Randall Stewart, p. 92.

26. *Works,* II, 502.

27. *Works*, II, 495.
28. *Works*, II, 501.
29. *Works*, II, 323.
30. *Works*, II, 346.
31. *Hawthorne's Last Phase*, p. 157.
32. "Hawthorne's Methods of Using his Source Materials," p. 312.
33. *Hawthorne's Last Phase*, p. 157.
34. *Letters . . . to William D. Ticknor*, II, 75.
35. For two examples see *The American Notebooks*, ed. Randall Stewart, pp. xxvii, 106, 130.
36. "The Two Hawthornes," *The Western*, I (June, 1875), 355.
37. *Hawthorne and his Circle* (New York and London: Harper & Brothers, 1903), p. 55.
38. Leland Schubert, *Hawthorne, the Artist*, p. 93.
39. C. T. Copeland, "Hawthorne's Use of his Materials," *The Critic*, XLV (July, 1904), 57.
40. *The Athenaeum*, No. 1230 (May 24, 1851), p. 547.
41. *Hawthorne's Last Phase*, p. 113. This is in particular reference to Draft "K" of *Septimius Felton*. See also pp. 118-19 and, for *The Dolliver Romance*, p. 137. The whole book is, it goes without saying, germane to this problem.
42. *Works*, I, 263.
43. *Works*, I, 270.
44. This tale can be compared in its meaning to "The Wedding Knell," in which the two aged lovers, after casting aside all hope of temporal happiness, wed for eternity. The stories are roughly contemporaneous; "The Wedding Knell" was probably written early in 1835 and "Dr. Heidegger's Experiment" in the Autumn of 1836.
45. *Septimius Felton* was written between 1861 and 1863; *The Dolliver Romance*, 1863-64. See E. H. Davidson, *Hawthorne's Last Phase*, p. vii.
46. *The American Notebooks*, ed. Randall Stewart, p. 101 (1842).
47. *Septimius Felton*, in *Works*, XI, 340-41.
48. *Hawthorne's Last Phase*, p. 82.
49. *Works*, XI, 404-13.
50. Quoted in *Nathaniel Hawthorne and his Wife*, II, 330.
51. *The Power of Blackness. Hawthorne, Poe, Melville* (New York: Alfred A. Knopf, 1958), p. 46.
52. *Works*, I, 77, 81. Mrs. Q. D. Leavis has brilliantly analyzed this tale, *op. cit.*, 185-95.
53. *Works*, I, 50-51.
54. In this discussion of "The Gentle Boy" I am generally indebted to Louise Dauner's study, "The 'Case' of Tobias Pearson: Hawthorne and the Ambiguities," *AL*, XXI (January, 1950), 464-72, though I by no means accept all her conclusions.

55. *Works,* I, 125-26.

56. My analysis of this tale is heavily indebted to that of R. R. Male in "The Dual Aspects of Evil in 'Rappaccini's Daughter'," *PMLA,* LXIX (March, 1954), 99-109.

57. "The Dual Aspects of Evil in 'Rappaccini's Daughter'," p. 107.

58. *Works,* VI, 247.

CHAPTER V: *Hawthorne and the Comic Spirit*

1. *The Flowering of New England, 1815-1865* (New York: The Modern Library, 1936), p. 223.

2. *Love Letters of Nathaniel Hawthorne* (2 vols.; Chicago: The Society of the Dofobs, 1907). The text of these letters is not absolutely trustworthy in this edition. In addition to some careless misdating, some of the letters have been bowdlerized to conform to the editors' standards of decorum. See Randall Stewart, "Letters to Sophia," *Huntington Library Quarterly,* VII (August, 1944), 387-95.

3. *Love Letters,* I, 223-24 (October 4, 1840).

4. *Love Letters,* II, 73-74 (January 20, 1842).

5. Randall Stewart has quoted this letter partially in *Nathaniel Hawthorne: A Biography,* p. 55; Edward Wagenknecht, following Stewart, has quoted it in *Nathaniel Hawthorne, Man and Writer,* pp. 54-55.

6. See R. H. Fogle, *Hawthorne's Fiction: The Light and the Dark,* H. H. Waggoner, *Hawthorne, a Critical Study,* and most important, R. R. Male, *Hawthorne's Tragic Vision* (Austin, Texas: University of Texas Press, 1957). This work discusses Hawthorne as a writer concerned basically with the problem of moral growth, who sees tragedy as an inevitable fact of human experience. Short studies of Hawthorne as a tragic writer also abound. In my opinion the best of these is Louise Dauner's "The 'Case' of Tobias Pearson," *op. cit.,* which, with particular reference to "The Gentle Boy," develops a general theory of Hawthornean tragedy.

7. "The Theme of Isolation in Hawthorne," *The Personalist,* XXXII (Winter, 1951), 59. Though this definition of tragedy may seem somewhat overly simple, Abel's distinction between tragedy and pathos is often overlooked and should be emphasized.

8. *Personal Recollections of Nathaniel Hawthorne* (New York: Harper & Brothers, 1893), p. 85.

9. *Hawthorne,* pp. 41-42.

10. *The Snow-Image,* in *Works,* III, 583.

11. *Works,* VII, 56-57.

12. *The American Notebooks,* ed. Randall Stewart, p. 101.

13. *The American Notebooks,* ed. Randall Stewart, p. 21. Constance Rourke has stumbled upon Hawthorne's fondness for the ludicrous,

which has left her rather puzzled. In common with most critics, she
attributes more high seriousness to Hawthorne than the facts
actually warrant, though she notes his interest in "odd and salient
characters" and even suggests that "his natural inclinations seem to
have been toward comedy," however much he may have suppressed
them in his art. *American Humor. A Study of the National Character*
(New York: Harcourt, Brace and Company), p. 186.

14. *Works*, V, 393.

15. *Works*, II, 305.

16. *Works*, IV, 46-47.

17. Quoted by Bridge in *Personal Recollections*, pp. 96-97. The
letter is dated April 1, 1844; the italics are Hawthorne's.

18. "Hawthorne and his Mosses," in Willard Thorp, ed., *Herman
Melville. Representative Selections* (New York: The American Book
Company, 1938), pp. 330-32.

19. *The American Notebooks*, ed. Randall Stewart, p. 98 (June 1,
1842).

20. *Passages from the American Note-Books*, in *Works*, IX, 110.

21. *Passages from the American Note-Books*, in *Works*, IX, 21.

22. See above, p. 103. My discussion of "Ethan Brand" is
much indebted to Professor Reilly's perceptive study.

23. *The American Notebooks*, ed. Randall Stewart, p. 106.

24. *The American Notebooks*, ed. Randall Stewart, p. 40 (July 30,
1838).

25. *Hawthorne's Tragic Vision*, p. 145.

26. The distinction is Hawthorne's. "It is only one-eyed people
who love to advise, or have any spontaneous promptitude of action.
When a man opens both his eyes, he generally sees about as many
reasons for acting in any one way as in any other, and quite as
many for acting in neither; and is therefore likely to leave his friends
to regulate their own conduct, and also to remain quiet as regards
his especial affairs till necessity shall prick him onward." He is
speaking particularly of his own unfitness, because of his "two-eyed"
unwillingness to advise, for a consular position, but the distinction has,
I think, a general relevance in his thought. See *Our Old Home*, in
Works, VII, 46-47.

27. *Works*, V, 599.

28. *Works*, V, 469.

29. The letter is published in part in the Introductory Note to
Our Old Home, in *Works*, VII, 11.

30. *A Study of Hawthorne* (Boston: James R. Osgood and Company, 1876), p. 242.

31. *Works*, V, 307-8.

32. *Works*, III, 198.

33. *Works*, VI, 494-95.

A Selected Bibliography

The following bibliography makes no pretense at being a comprehensive survey. It contains only those works to which specific reference has been made in the Notes and those to which I am generally indebted, though the indebtedness has not been acknowledged otherwise. My own bibliographical research is based largely on Walter Blair's "Hawthorne," in *Eight American Authors: A Review of Research and Criticism* (New York: The Modern Language Association of America, 1956), pp. 100-52, to which work I refer the reader.

ABEL, DARREL. "The Devil in Boston," *Philological Quarterly*, XXXII (October, 1953), 366-81.
————. "Hawthorne's Hester," *College English*, XIII (March, 1952), 303-9.
————. "Hawthorne's House of Tradition," *South Atlantic Quarterly*, LII (October, 1953), 561-78.
————. "Hawthorne's Skepticism about Social Reform: With Especial Reference to *The Blithedale Romance*," *University of Kansas City Review*, XIX (Spring, 1953), 181-93.
————. "A Masque of Love and Death," *University of Toronto Quarterly*, XXIII (October, 1953), 9-25.
————. "The Theme of Isolation in Hawthorne," *The Personalist*, XXXII (Winter and Spring, 1951), 42-59, 182-90.
ADKINS, NELSON F. "The Early Projected Works of Nathaniel Hawthorne," *Papers of the Bibliographical Society of America*, XXXIX (April-June, 1945), 119-55.
BACON, THEODORE. *Delia Bacon. A Biographical Sketch*. Boston and New York: Houghton, Mifflin and Company, 1888.
BICKNELL, JOHN W. "*The Marble Faun* Reconsidered," *University of Kansas City Review*, XX (Spring, 1954), 193-99.
BIER, JESSE. "Hawthorne on the Romance: His Prefaces Related and Examined," *Modern Philology*, LIII (August, 1955), 17-24.
BLAIR, WALTER. "Color, Light, and Shadow in Hawthorne's Fiction," *New England Quarterly*, XV (March, 1942), 74-94.
BLODGETT, HAROLD. "Hawthorne as Poetry Critic: Six Unpublished Letters to Lewis Mansfield," *American Literature*, XII (May, 1940), 173-84.
BOEWE, CHARLES. "Rappaccini's Garden," *American Literature*, XXX (March, 1958), 37-49.
BRIDGE, HORATIO. *Personal Recollections of Nathaniel Hawthorne*. New York: Harper & Brothers, 1893.

BROOKS, VAN WYCK. *The Flowering of New England, 1815-1865.* New York: The Modern Library, 1936.

BROWNE, NINA ELIZA. *A Bibliography of Nathaniel Hawthorne.* Boston and New York: Houghton, Mifflin and Company, 1905.

BROWNELL, WILLIAM CRARY. "Hawthorne," in *American Prose Masters. Cooper—Hawthorne—Emerson—Poe—Lowell—Henry James.* New York: Charles Scribner's Sons, 1909, pp. 63-130.

CANTWELL, ROBERT. "Hawthorne and Delia Bacon," *American Quarterly,* I (Winter, 1949), 343-60.

————. *Nathaniel Hawthorne: The American Years.* New York, Toronto: Rinehart & Company, Incorporated, 1948.

CHANDLER, ELIZABETH LATHROP. *A Study of the Sources of the Tales and Romances Written by Nathaniel Hawthorne before 1853, Smith College Studies in Modern Language,* Vol. VII (July, 1926).

[CHORLEY, HENRY FOTHERGILL.] Review of *The House of the Seven Gables, The Athenaeum,* No. 1230 (May 24, 1851), pp. 545-47.

COHEN, B. BERNARD. "'Eternal Truth': A Study of Nathaniel Hawthorne's Philosophy." Unpublished doctoral thesis in the library of the Indiana University.

————. "Hawthorne's 'Mrs. Bullfrog' and *The Rambler,*" *Philological Quarterly,* XXXII (October, 1953), 382-87.

COPELAND, CHARLES TOWNSEND. "Hawthorne's Use of his Materials," *The Critic,* XLV (July, 1904), 56-60.

COWLEY, MALCOLM. "One Hundred Years Ago: Hawthorne Set a Great New Pattern," *New York Herald Tribune Books* (August 6, 1950), pp. 1, 13.

CREWS, FREDERICK C. "A New Reading of *The Blithedale Romance,*" *American Literature,* XXIX (May, 1957), 147-70.

CURL, VEGA. *Pasteboard Masks. Fact as Spiritual Symbol in the Novels of Hawthorne and Melville.* Cambridge, Massachusetts: Harvard University Press, 1931.

DAUNER, LOUISE. "The 'Case' of Tobias Pearson: Hawthorne and the Ambiguities," *American Literature,* XXI (January, 1950), 464-72.

DAVIDSON, FRANK. "Toward a Re-evaluation of *The Blithedale Romance,*" *New England Quarterly,* XXV (September, 1952), 374-83.

DICHMANN, MARY E. "Hawthorne's 'Prophetic Pictures'," *American Literature,* XXIII (May, 1951), 188-202.

DOUBLEDAY, NEAL FRANK. "The Theme of Hawthorne's 'Fancy's Show Box'," *American Literature,* X (November, 1938), 341-43.

EISINGER, CHESTER E. "Hawthorne as Champion of the Middle Way," *New England Quarterly,* XXVII (March, 1954), 27-52.

FAIRBANKS, HENRY G. "Sin, Free Will and 'Pessimism' in Hawthorne," *PMLA,* LXXI (December, 1956), 975-89.

FAUST, BERTHA. *Hawthorne's Contemporaneous Reputation, a Study of*

Literary Opinion in America and England, 1828-1864. Philadelphia: The University of Pennsylvania, 1939.

FEIDELSON, CHARLES, JR. *Symbolism and American Literature.* Chicago: University of Chicago Press, 1953.

FICK, FATHER LEONARD JOHN. *The Light Beyond: A Study of Hawthorne's Theology.* Westminster, Maryland: Newman Press, 1955.

FIELDS, JAMES THOMAS. *Hawthorne.* Boston: James R. Osgood and Company, 1876.

FOGLE, RICHARD HARTER. "Ambiguity and Clarity in Hawthorne's 'Young Goodman Brown'," *New England Quarterly,* XVIII (December, 1945), 448-65.

————. *Hawthorne's Fiction: The Light and the Dark.* Norman, Oklahoma: University of Oklahoma Press, 1952.

————. "The World and the Artist: A Study of Hawthorne's 'The Artist of the Beautiful'," *Tulane Studies in English,* I (1949), 31-52.

GERBER, JOHN C. "Form and Content in The Scarlet Letter," *New England Quarterly,* XVII (March, 1944), 25-55.

GWYNN, FREDERICK L. "Hawthorne's 'Rappaccini's Daughter'," *Nineteenth-Century Fiction,* VII (December, 1952), 217-19.

HAWTHORNE, JULIAN. *Hawthorne and his Circle.* New York and London: Harper & Brothers, 1903.

————. *Nathaniel Hawthorne and his Wife: A Biography,* 2 vols. New York: Houghton, Mifflin and Company, 1884.

HAWTHORNE, NATHANIEL. *The American Notebooks by Nathaniel Hawthorne,* ed. Randall Stewart. New Haven, Connecticut: Yale University Press, 1932.

————. *The Complete Novels and Selected Tales of Nathaniel Hawthorne,* ed. Norman Holmes Pearson. New York: The Modern Library, 1937.

————. *The Complete Works of Nathaniel Hawthorne, with Introductory Notes by George Parsons Lathrop,* ed. George Parsons Lathrop. 13 vols. Boston and New York: Houghton, Mifflin and Company, 1882 (The Riverside Edition).

————. *The English Notebooks by Nathaniel Hawthorne,* ed. Randall Stewart. New York: The Modern Language Association of America; London: Oxford University Press, 1941.

————. *Hawthorne's Last Phase,* ed. Edward Hutchins Davidson. New Haven, Connecticut: Yale University Press, 1949.

————. "Hawthorne's 'Spectator'," ed. Elizabeth Lathrop Chandler, *New England Quarterly,* IV (April, 1931), 288-307.

————. *Letters of Hawthorne to William D. Ticknor, 1851-1864.* 2 vols. Newark, New Jersey: The Carteret Book Club, 1910.

————. "Letters to Sophia," ed. Randall Stewart, *Huntington Library Quarterly,* VII (August, 1944), 387-95.

——. *Love Letters of Nathaniel Hawthorne.* 2 vols. Chicago: The Society of the Dofobs, 1907.

——. *The Portable Hawthorne,* ed. Malcolm Cowley. New York: The Viking Press, 1948.

HAYFORD, HARRISON. "Hawthorne, Melville, and the Sea," *New England Quarterly,* XIX (December, 1946), 435-52.

HEILMAN, R. B. "Hawthorne's 'The Birthmark': Science as Religion," *South Atlantic Quarterly,* XLVIII (October, 1949), 575-83.

KESSELRING, MARION L. *Hawthorne's Reading, 1828-1850. A Transcription and Identification of Titles Recorded in the Charge-Books of the Salem Athenaeum.* New York: The New York Public Library, 1949.

LATHROP, GEORGE PARSONS. *A Study of Hawthorne.* Boston: James R. Osgood and Company, 1876.

LEAVIS, QUEENIE D. "Hawthorne as Poet," *Sewanee Review,* LIX (Spring and Summer, 1951), 179-205, 426-58.

LEVIN, HARRY. *The Power of Blackness. Hawthorne, Poe, Melville.* New York: Alfred A. Knopf, 1958.

MAGGINIS, MARY AMELIA. "Hawthorne's Comments on the Arts as Evidence of an Aesthetic Theory." Unpublished doctoral thesis in the library of the University of North Carolina.

MALE, ROY R., JR. "The Dual Aspects of Evil in 'Rappaccini's Daughter'," *PMLA,* LXIX (March, 1954), 99-109.

——. " 'From the Innermost Germ': The Organic Principle in Hawthorne's Fiction," *ELH,* XX (September, 1953), 218-36.

——. "Hawthorne and the Concept of Sympathy," *PMLA* LXVIII (March, 1953), 138-49.

——. *Hawthorne's Tragic Vision.* Austin, Texas: University of Texas Press, 1957.

MATTHIESSEN, F. O. *American Renaissance: Art and Expression in the Age of Emerson and Whitman.* London, Toronto, New York: Oxford University Press, 1941.

MELVILLE, HERMAN. "Hawthorne and his Mosses," in *Herman Melville. Representative Selections, with Introduction, Bibliography, and Notes,* ed. Willard Thorp. New York, *et al.*: The American Book Company, 1938, pp. 327-45.

NEWMAN, FRANKLIN B. " 'My Kinsman, Major Molineaux' [*sic*]: An Interpretation," *University of Kansas City Review,* XXI (March, 1955), 203-12.

OREL, HAROLD. "The Double Symbol," *American Literature,* XXIII (March, 1951), 1-6.

PEABODY, ELIZABETH P. "The Two Hawthornes," *The Western,* I (June, 1875), 352-59.

PEARCE, ROY HARVEY. "Hawthorne and the Twilight of Romance," *Yale Review,* XXXVII (March, 1948), 487-506.

PRITCHARD, JOHN PAUL. *Return to the Fountains: Some Classical*

Sources of American Criticism. Durham, North Carolina: Duke University Press, 1942.

REILLY, CYRIL A. "On the Dog's Chasing His Own Tail in 'Ethan Brand'," *PMLA*, LXVIII (December, 1953), 975-81.

ROURKE, CONSTANCE. *American Humor. A Study of the National Character*. New York: Harcourt, Brace and Company, 1931.

SCHILLER, ANDREW. "The Moment and the Endless Voyage: A Study of Hawthorne's 'Wakefield'," *Diameter*, I (March, 1951), 7-12.

SCHNEIDER, HERBERT WALLACE. *The Puritan Mind*. New York: Henry Holt and Company, 1930.

SCHUBERT, LELAND. *Hawthorne, the Artist: Fine-Art Devices in Fiction*. Chapel Hill, North Carolina: The University of North Carolina Press, 1944.

SHROEDER, JOHN W. " 'That Inward Sphere': Notes on Hawthorne's Heart Imagery and Symbolism," *PMLA*, LXV (March, 1950), 106-19.

STEIN, WILLIAM BYSSHE. *Hawthorne's Faust: A Study of the Devil Archetype*. Gainesville, Florida: University of Florida Press, 1953.

STEWART, RANDALL. "Hawthorne and the Civil War," *Studies in Philology*, XXXIV (January, 1937), 91-106.

————. "Hawthorne and Politics: Unpublished Letters to William B. Pike," *New England Quarterly*, V (April, 1932), 237-63.

————. "Hawthorne in England: The Patriotic Motive in the Note-Books," *New England Quarterly*, VIII (March, 1935), 3-13.

————. "Hawthorne's Last Illness and Death," *More Books*, XIX (October, 1944), 303-13.

————. "The Hawthornes at the Wayside, 1860-1864," *More Books*, XIX (September, 1944), 263-79.

————. "Melville and Hawthorne," *South Atlantic Quarterly*, LI (July, 1952), 436-46.

————. *Nathaniel Hawthorne: A Biography*. New Haven, Connecticut: Yale University Press, 1948.

————. "Recollections of Hawthorne by His Sister Elizabeth," *American Literature*, XVI (January, 1945), 316-31.

TROLLOPE, ANTHONY. "The Genius of Nathaniel Hawthorne," *North American Review*, CXXIX (September, 1879), 203-22.

TURNER, ARLIN. "Hawthorne's Methods of Using his Source Materials," in *Studies for William A. Read*, eds. Nathaniel M. Caffee and Thomas A. Kirby. University, Louisiana: The Louisiana State University Press, 1940, pp. 301-12.

WAGENKNECHT, EDWARD. *Nathaniel Hawthorne. Man and Writer*. London, New York: Oxford University Press, 1961.

WAGGONER, HYATT H. *Hawthorne, a Critical Study*. Cambridge, Massachusetts: Harvard University Press, 1955.

WALCUTT, CHARLES CHILD. "*The Scarlet Letter* and Its Modern Critics," *Nineteenth-Century Fiction*, VII (March, 1953), 251-64.

Index

"Mrs. Bullfrog," 27, 29-30, 31
"Morning Watch, The"; see Mansfield, Lewis
Mosses From an Old Manse, 144-46
"My Kinsman, Major Molyneux," 31, 32-33, 92, 125-26

Novel; see Romance, and novel compared

"Ode on a Grecian Urn," 40
"Old Apple Dealer, The," 103-5, 106
Oriental Tale; see Eastern Tale
Our Old Home, 138

Pierce, Franklin, 14, 15-16, 150-51
Pilgrim's Progress, The, 87-89, 92
Platonism, H's, 13-14, 16, 17, 23-24, 27, 36-44, 47-49, 157-61
"Procession of Life, The," 26-27, 32, 33, 92
"Prophetic Pictures, The," 28, 42-45, 85
Providence, 13-15, 16, 18, 22-23, 48-49
"P's Correspondence," 41-42, 46

"Rappaccini's Daughter," 46, 52-53, 74, 95, 114, 126-28
Rasselas, 75, 76-78, 92
"Roger Malvin's Burial," 92
Romance, and novel compared, 50-56, 58, 60-62, 64-65, 69-70, 80

Scarlet Letter, The, 21-22, 59-62, 63, 85, 95-98, 99, 101-3, 108-9, 110, 112, 120, 125, 128-29, 130, 137, 152-53, 160
"Select Party, A," 41-42, 86, 90, 92
Septimius Felton, 114-19, 148
"Shaker Bridal, The," 122
Shelley, Percy Bysshe, 17, 161
"Sights from a Steeple," 42
"Snow-Image, The," 47
"'Spectator', The," 30
Stoddard, Richard Henry, 117-18
"Sunday at Home," 59
"Sylph Etherege," 41

"Threefold Destiny, The," 74-78, 92
Transcendentalists, 17, 52-53, 87-89
Trollope, Anthony, 51, 54
Twice-Told Tales, Preface, 56, 63

Unpardonable Sin, The, 34, 103, 129, 146-47

Vathek, 75

"Wakefield," 84, 101
"Wedding Knell, The," 85, 118, 122-23, 146
Wonder-Book, A, 65-70, 142-43

"Young Goodman Brown," 18-19, 31-32, 33, 77, 92, 146